T0196346

A TIME to SHARE

NORBERT WEINBERG

authorHOUSE®

AuthorHouse™
1663 Liberty Drive
Bloomington, IN 47403
www.authorhouse.com
Phone: 1 (800) 839-8640

Authorized (King James) Version (AKJV)
KJV reproduced by permission of Cambridge University Press, the Crown's patentee in the UK.

New American Standard Bible (NASB)
*Copyright © 1960, 1962, 1963, 1968, 1971, 1972, 1973,
1975, 1977, 1995 by The Lockman Foundation*

Published by AuthorHouse 06/27/2017

ISBN: 978-1-5246-9656-6 (sc)
ISBN: 978-1-5246-9654-2 (hc)
ISBN: 978-1-5246-9655-9 (e)

Library of Congress Control Number: 2017909312

Print information available on the last page.

Certain stock imagery © Thinkstock.

This book is printed on acid-free paper.

Table of Contents

Introduction..xv

Childhood Memories

The first part of our life is controlled by our parents, the second part by our children (and grandchildren!). (Rabbi Norbert Weinberg)

The Best of Both Worlds.. 3
A Father's Blessing.. 4
Your Mother's Torah 6
Be Prepared... 8
Learning to Add.. 10
My First Funeral 11
The Demise of the Family Doctor.................................... 14
On Ancestry...17
Was I Baptized?...19
Countdown for Cheesecake... 20
I Only Eat at Home 22

The Cycle of Life

Everything has its season and there is a time for everything under the heaven. A time to be born and a time to die…a time to weep and a time to laugh…a time to mourn and a time to dance…a time for peace and a time for war. (Ecclesiastes 3:1-8)

A Time for all Occasions.. 27
Nothing New... 29

No Tallit Until Marriage.. 30
Feting the Bride and Groom 32
Dancing to the Chuppa.. 34
No Mirrors at Shiva 36
Of Pebbles and Boulders 38
One View of Hell.. 39
Kaddish on Festivals 40

The Jewish Calendar

*What kind of a summer does a Jew have? Seven weeks
he counts (the Omer), three weeks (before Tisha B'Av)
he cries and four weeks he blows (the Shofar) - and the
summer is over.* (Dr. Seligmann Weinberg, my father)

The Most Important Month of the Year.................................... 45
The Power of Leadership 47
Why is This Passover Different? 50
Thirty-Three Days? 52
A Day of Distinction.. 55
Sadness on Rosh Chodesh?.. 57
How Many Fast Days? 59
Napoleon and the Holy Temple.. 62
A Tisha B'Av Concert... 64

Rabbinic Musings

*If everyone likes the rabbi, he is not a rabbi.
If no one likes the rabbi, he is not a mensch.*
(Rabbi Israel Salanter – 1809-1883)

Is the Rabbi a Teacher?.. 67
The Rabbi's Complaint 69
Stretching it a Bit 71
What Goes Around Comes Around 72
A Potential Pitfall... 75
Welcome! 77
A Cup of Coffee with God?... 79

A Movable Synagogue 81
Which Mountain is Holier? 83

Jewish Concepts

If someone was determined to perform a mitzva
and was prevented from doing so, Scripture credits
him as if he had performed it. (Berachot 6a)

On Teleology 87
Who Turned on the Lights? 90
Love can be a Halachic Imperative 92
No Daily Blessing 93
The Rich Need Blessing 95
The Power of a Blessing or Curse 98
But I Didn't Do It! 100
A Case for Teshuva 102
Lead us into Temptation 103
Bagel Seeds 105
Glatt Versus Super-Glatt 107
Tallit Over the Head 109
What is Techelet? 111
Out of Line 113
Is the Kippa Holy? 114
Spiritual Blood Pressure 116
A Tzadik and a Chasid 117
Fleecing the Congregation..119
That Controversial Sheitel 121
A Taste of Responsa 123
The Hidden Matza... 128
Jewish Humor 129

Torah and Talmudic Insights

Scripture states that Adam was created from the dust of the earth. Which part of the earth? From every sector, to prevent any man from saying, "The world was created for my sake." (Sanhedrin 38b)

***

Rabbi Yochanan Ben Zakkai said, "If you have a sapling in your hand and are told, 'Look the Messiah is coming,' you should first plant the sapling and then go on to welcome the Messiah." (Avot de'Rabbi Natan 31)

The Garden of Eden Exists 133

What was the First Sin? 134

Only One Commandment 136

"And God Blessed Abraham With Everything" (Genesis 24:1) 138

The Goal is Cloaked in Mystery 140

"Little" Isaac 142

Where Was Sarah? 144

The House of Israel 146

Rebecca Revisited 148

"And the Boys Grew" 150

Who is This "Ish"? 151

A Positive Ending? 154

The Grave by the Wayside 156

Moses: Personification of Humility 158

Women in the Exodus 161

Three Days of Darkness 164

When Did Moses Break the Tablets? 166

The Donkey That Spoke 168

"I Awaken the Dawn" (Psalms 108:2) 171

We Are All Job 173

A Share For All 176

Do as I Say 178

Rabbi Meir and Women 180

What Will My Neighbors Say?..182
Seize the Moment 183

Jewish History and the Land of Israel
*"My claim to being Jewish is not because my
parents are Jewish - it is because my grandchildren
are Jewish."* (Rabbi Norbert Weinberg)

Genesis of Anti-Semitism 187
Those "Brave" Anti-Semites 189
Encourage the Arab Boycott 193
Where is Babylonia? 197
The Unique Egg.. 201
Jewish Leadership... 204
The Land of Israel 207
A Land Flowing with Milk and Honey 209
My Own Israel Miracle 211
Lest We Forget..213
One Big Family...215

Observations
*"If you would like to think about numbers, consider how
many snowflakes it takes to produce a huge blizzard. Then
marvel at the fact that each snowflake is reputed to have its
own unique shape and design."* (Rabbi Norbert Weinberg)

Sitting in the House of God 219
Something Does Not Compute.. 221
Mirror, Mirror on the Wall 222
The Power of Possession 224
Gesundheit.. 225
Easy Does It.. 227
Old or New... 228

The Animal World

*"If one person tells you that you have the ears of a donkey,
pay no attention to him. If two people tell you, prepare
a saddle for yourself." (Midrash Rabba; Bereshit 45)*

A Personal Concern... 233
Breakfast with a Kitten 235
Lessons from the Animal World.. 236

Final Thought

*"May the Lord bless you from Zion; may you see the good of
Jerusalem all the days of your life; and may you live to see
your children's children. Peace be on Israel!" (Psalms 128)*

Of Children and Peace.. 241

Acknowledgements

Since we are limited to only two ears and one mouth, I have always tried to follow the excellent advice to listen carefully and speak only half as much as I hear. This is especially pertinent when authoring short articles which are a summation of the collective knowledge that I have received and an attempt to project and relay this information as I have perceived it. Individual recognition of this vast exposure would be an exercise in futility. This, however, does not detract from my gratitude to my entire family, former congregants and innumerable friends who have enriched, and continue to enrich, my knowledge and broaden my horizons.

I am reminded of the story of a person who looked everywhere for a pot of gold and discovered it in his own backyard! When I discussed my literary plans with my daughter, Shira Schreier, I realized what a vast background she had in this field. Happily, she took over the task of bringing my manuscript to fruition and the book moved ahead at full speed, reflecting her expertise and literary perception.

Helpers included quite a few generations. My daughter, Rena Rossman, carefully read large parts of the text, as did her daughter, Tzippora. These efforts greatly added to the quality and success of the book. There were many others who offered their help but, as I said, it would be too difficult to list them all. My deepest appreciation goes to all, individually and collectively.

In her quiet manner, my wife, Susan, would offer excellent comments at various intervals. Her suggestions were always accepted and greatly elevated the quality of the book.

To each and every one, my deepest and sincerest appreciation. I hope the reader will enjoy the book as much I did in preparing it.

Norbert Weinberg
Efrat, Israel
May, 2017

Dedication

Since this book is a composite of knowledge compiled throughout my life from my parents and relatives with me and beyond, I dedicate this book to them all, especially the huge group of grandchildren and great grandchildren who are enriching every aspect of my life.

Introduction

O ne of the greatest advances in sharing the printed word was the development of personal publishing. Before the advent of this industry, unless an aspiring author had access to ample funding, he/she had no recourse but to submit his/her manuscript to the dubious mercies of the editors of a publishing house. The usual inevitable result of this effort, after a long period of waiting, was a rejection slip. Perhaps, if luck would have it, the reviewer might have suggested a rewrite, which sent the excited author back to his/her desk to engage in drawn out revisions. More often than not, these efforts ended in eventual rejections. Only the tiniest percentage of these budding authors managed to navigate through all the hurdles and ultimately have their works see the light of day.

Of course it was not the fault of the publishers. It takes a great deal of investment to publish a book and they had to try to recoup their expenses through sales. It seems to me to be a very tricky business and if I were a publisher who was in the slightest doubt about the success of a manuscript, I would give myself no choice but to reject it.

The next step in the development of authors bringing their works to light was called "vanity publishing." I consider this term to be nothing less than insulting to the myriad of original thinkers who were driven by an intense desire to turn their thoughts into print. There is no more vanity in this craving than for a medical student to perform his first operation. Happily, it did not take long for this new venture to rapidly succeed and to ultimately be known simply as "self-publishing." It now became possible for anyone to convert his thoughts into print, even if the production of the book was not followed by spectacular sales. I see little vanity in this endeavor. It is almost akin to the longing to give birth. Sometimes the book might be shared by only family and friends but, above all, it is the supreme achievement of the author who gave tangible expression to his innermost thoughts.

I was privileged to have my first book produced by the Bloch Publishing Company quite a few years ago. It was an indescribable thrill of completion that catapulted me into attempting more of the same. Although I won second prize for a short story about the sale of *chametz*, I soon realized that if I was going to keep moving ahead, it would have to be on my own. I was simply not willing to continue to make submissions and wait for months for probable rejections. I also noticed that the field of self-publishing seemed to have grown so much that the costs were manageable and that many competitive companies had joined the literary scene. I have followed this path and while the books that I published were far from best-sellers, they mean a great deal to me.

It should come as no surprise that, as a rabbi for quite some years, I have delivered many sermons in the hope that they contained original and meaningful thoughts. When engaged in teaching Torah to children and adults, new ideas constantly spring to life. I have always tried to hold on to these ideas and never let them go. Notes on slips of paper accumulated. This work, and a few previous books, are an attempt to formalize these ideas and share them with a wider audience.

There is one problem in such an endeavor. How can I possibly know which concepts, over the course of years, are totally mine and which I may have heard from or been influenced by others?

The Talmud teaches: "Whoever reports a saying in the name of the one who said it brings redemption to the world" (Megilla 15a).

From the time that I started saying prayers next to my father as a little boy until the present moment, I have been blessed with teachers, rabbis, students, family and friends, all of whom have greatly enriched me with their Torah treasures through word and deed. It would be totally impossible for me to quote each of them.

Therefore, I would like to convey my deepest gratitude to each of them and happily declare that all that I have written is an accumulation of what I have learned and continue to glean from them. Their individual names are far too many to list, but if they read this, they will know I mean them.

Hopefully, the strength and scope of this credit will be so strong that it will hasten the promised Redemption.

All that I have received and the little that I may have added is shared in this book with the deepest love and affection that only the Torah can inspire.

- Norbert Weinberg

CHILDHOOD MEMORIES

The first part of our life is controlled by our parents,
the second part by our children (and grandchildren!).
(Rabbi Norbert Weinberg)

The Best of Both Worlds

I have a distinct memory of my early youth in Germany. It happened at the end of the Sabbath services on Friday evenings when the *Kiddush* was chanted. The children would line up in two rows. One line was to receive the traditional blessing from the rabbi, who would place his hands on each child's head and murmur a short prayer. The children on the other line received a small cup containing some of the *Kiddush* wine.

The choice between these two lines presented a weekly dilemma for me, despite my young age. Of course, I very much wanted to be blessed by the revered rabbi, but the prospect of missing out on that delicious wine did not appeal to me at all.

I managed to solve the problem in a somewhat ingenious manner. I positioned myself at the very front of one of the two rows. As soon as I received either the blessing or the wine, I quickly rushed to the other row in time to receive my second bonus.

Thus, early in life, I learned the lesson that it *can* be possible to achieve the best of both worlds!

A Father's Blessing

To the best of my memory, it was the custom of my father to bless us on Friday evenings *after* the meal. This certainly is not the prevalent custom. Most of the parents I know bless their children upon coming home from the synagogue. When asked about my custom which puts the blessing off until the very end of the meal, I used to be somewhat reluctant to defend my father's timing. I was not sure if his practice was predicated upon specific reasons or perhaps he was just relaxed and waiting for an opportune moment later in the evening.

One day, as I was reading Nachmanides (The Ramban - Rabbi Moses ben Nachman 1194-1270), an entire new vista on this matter was revealed to me.

The following are his words:

> As for Isaac's saying that he would bless Esau after he had prepared the savory meats for him, that was not a reward or a recompense for the food. Instead, he wanted to derive some benefit from him so that his very soul would be bound up in his at the time that he brought him the food, so that he would then bless him with a complete desire and a perfect will. Perhaps Isaac discerned in himself that following the meal, his soul would be delighted and joyous, and then the Holy Spirit would come upon him.

When we come home from services on Friday night, we are in a mood of anticipation. The week of rushing is over and we are probably hungry and eager to sit around our dining room table laden with all the Sabbath delicacies. Once the meal is over, however, our feelings reflect satisfaction and fulfillment – the best time for blessing. In fact, the entire concept of *Oneg Shabbat* (enjoyment of the Sabbath) is based upon the pleasure we receive from the food and delicacies, which are among the defining components of this day.

We even find this concept expressed in the Grace After Meals when we say, "You shall eat and you shall be satisfied and you shall bless" (Deuteronomy 6:11).

So perhaps my father's custom to bless us after the meal was not the result of a chance postponement. He may even have received this as a tradition from his father, who was a very knowledgeable rabbi. In any event, there is certainly enough confirmation to support his custom on the basis of all this evidence.

For my part, I have followed this tradition with my children with the greatest satisfaction.

Your Mother's Torah

" Listen, my son, to the instruction of your father and do not forsake the Torah (teaching) of your mother" (Proverbs 1:8).

It is quite amazing when I reflect upon the influence these words have had and continue to have on my everyday activities.

Let me explain.

I remember that my mother did not remove flowers from the table on Shabbat.

As a result, I have always avoided moving flowers in a vase on the table on Shabbat. A review of the laws governing this matter would, it would seem, find no objection to moving them. A potted plant, on the other hand, should not be moved because as soon as it would be exposed to a light shaft, growth would automatically take place. Thus, the mover would be in violation of one of the thirty-nine prohibited Sabbath activities, namely *zeriya* (planting). This does not apply to cut flowers in a vase, since their growth has terminated. There are many nuances to these rules, but I have stated the accepted ruling as expressed by the *Rema* 336:11 (Rabbi Moshe Isserlis 1520-1572).

Now one would think that having gained this information, there would be no problem for me to pick up and carry such a vase of flowers on or off the table. Yet, I have felt a consistent restraint and simply left the task for others. My wife doesn't even ask me to do it anymore.

One might say that from a technical and logical point, I am very foolish and that may be true. Yet, in this matter and quite a few others, the "Torah" which my mother has passed on to me is as powerful as the letter of the law. I don't know if she misunderstood the rule or if a rabbi advised her against moving flowers for some reason, but it doesn't really matter. This is something she did not do and therefore I choose not to do it either. I find it very hard to "forsake" the Torah of my mother.

There are many more such practices that I can think of. When I speak to people, I find that many others practice similar *minhagim (*customs).

Perhaps I can allow myself to end on a humorous note. The story is told of a great Talmudic sage who prepared a snack for himself in the kitchen. He mistakenly sliced a soft piece of cheese with a *fleishig (*meat) knife. At that very moment, his wife entered the kitchen and loudly screamed at him when she saw what had happened.

"Please, my dear, do not be upset," the Talmudic sage said soothingly. "It is really nothing. The Jewish law is quite clear on this. The cold knife and the cold cheese will not interact with each other."

Far from being placated, his wife shouted, "Out! You and your *Shulchan Aruch* (Code of Jewish law) will yet make my kitchen *treiff* (non-kosher)!"

Do not trifle with your mother's Torah.

Be Prepared

The major part of my bar mitzva training was undertaken by my father, who taught me the proper chanting of my Torah portion, *Vayishlach*. He was of the opinion that no mistake need ever be made by the one who publicly reads the Torah. It must be remembered that there are no vowels or musical notes to sustain the reader. Some people have a predisposition of mastering the reading quite quickly. In my case, it is a slow process and is only perfected by a great deal of repetition.

Nevertheless, because of my father's diligence and persistence, I delivered the reading without a flaw.

Trouble developed the following week. I was part of a "junior congregation" which was composed of pre-bar mitzva boys and teenagers who conducted their own service on an abridged level. The Torah readings were much shorter than those of the adult congregation. They consisted only of the first portion of the weekly selection.

No one had been appointed to read the Torah that Shabbat and the rabbi asked me to do it. I told him that I was unprepared and would not be able to comply. He became extremely insistent and said that he would stand by my side and prompt me as I went along. I finally gave in and began to chant the text. It was a disaster. I did not pronounce the words correctly and I certainly did not know the proper musical cantillations.

Unbeknown to me, my father was standing outside the door and was a witness to the entire debacle. When he called me out, he was quite angry and told me in no uncertain terms that I was never to read the Torah in the future unless I was fully prepared.

In the meantime I learned that Rabbi Akiva was once invited to read the Torah and he declined on the grounds that he had not properly reviewed the text. Now I had little doubt that this great rabbi knew the Torah by heart. Yet, he felt that proper preparation was an essential prerequisite.

It was an important lesson for me and I have complied ever since. I also began to realize that the applications are even broader. Before plunging into anything, it is so much better if one is properly prepared.

Learning to Add

I have a clear recollection of this little incident that happened in Bad Nauheim, Germany, the city of my birth. I was four or five years old. My parents were in a room along with a number of other people. In an effort to show me off, I was asked to add the numbers five and five and tell everyone the result. I very carefully counted up to five and then continued with the numbers six and seven until I reached ten.

Amid general laughter, I was told that it was not necessary to start with number one; I could start with five and continue from there.

Perhaps I have not progressed very far from that revelation to this day. Not long ago, I acquired a backup disk for the data on my computer. Whenever I updated this information, I deleted everything on the disk and started all over again. Recently, I was informed that this was totally unnecessary, if not foolish. I simply had to copy the new data onto the existing information.

I have decided not to apply for the position of rocket scientist!

My First Funeral

O ne of the less than happy duties of my life as a rabbi has been officiating at funerals, an inevitable part of the life cycle of every community. Nevertheless, my first funeral, if it may be called that, goes back to the time long before I became a rabbi. In fact, it occurred around the time that my family and I came to America.

Entrance into the United States at the present time is much easier. Not only have past restrictions been greatly relaxed, but there is massive illegal immigration accompanied by heated discussions regarding the disposition of those who crossed the border illegally. For us, it was much more difficult.

Living in Germany before the outbreak of WWII, we were desperate to escape. In fact, my father had been incarcerated in the Buchenwald concentration camp for six weeks. Our hope was to be admitted as immigrants to America. There was a strict quota system at the time which allowed only a specific number of immigrants from various countries. Every candidate for entry had to prove financial responsibility. If he did not have the personal resources, he had to have a sponsor to legally assume this obligation. In other words, strict laws were extant to prevent the immigrant from becoming a ward of the state.

Unlike today, it was understood that English was the legal and accepted language of the country. Signs were only in English. It was the newcomer who had to make the effort of learning the language of the country that he had chosen. One of the requirements my father had to address in order to obtain his license to practice medicine was fluency in English. I remember him frequently going to the movies so that he could learn the nuances of spoken English.

The financial responsibility for my family was assumed by a Mr. Max Stern, the owner of Hartz Mountain pet foods. In later years, Yeshiva University's division of Stern College for Women was endowed by this great philanthropist. His interest in my family, as I understand it, stemmed from the fact that my father, a cardiologist in Germany, happened to have been the doctor of Max Stern's father. So when we arrived in America, Mr. Stern looked after all our immediate needs, which gave my father the opportunity to re-study for his medical examinations until he was finally licensed to again practice medicine.

One day, our family decided that we would like to have a bird as a pet. Everyone was in agreement and there was a great deal of anticipation. After purchasing the cage, sand and bird food, we contacted Mr. Stern and asked him if we might come to his office in order to purchase a canary. He graciously consented and told us that the cost of the bird would be five dollars. The price, even at that time, was very low and I suspect that the only reason he charged anything was so that we could maintain our dignity in making a purchase rather than receiving a charitable gift.

By a stroke of luck, I was chosen to go to downtown New York and purchase the new pet. I have a vague recollection of Mr. Stern being very cordial and accepting the five dollars which I handed to him with great seriousness, as if it was one of the larger transactions which he had negotiated that week. He also gave me detailed instructions regarding how to care for the bird.

For reasons unbeknown to me, the canary was named Moritz. Moritz made himself at home and seemed to be quite happy. At first, no sound emanated from him. After a few days, however, we were totally enthralled to hear the most delightful tunes emanating from his tiny throat. As his arias reached a crescendo, his little chest puffed out and his feathers seemed to double in size. His concerts began in the morning and continued for a good part of the day. In the evenings, we covered his cage with a cloth and he went to sleep for the night.

Little did we realize one morning that our little canary had regaled us with his last musical performance. We were very sad because it seemed to us that he knew us and that he sang his beautiful melodies just for us.

The question arose as to how to dispose of our now silenced friend. We certainly were not going to throw him into the garbage or even into some bush. My brother and I decided that a respectful burial was clearly indicated. We probably would not have felt that way had we been older, but young people are still free of accepted mores and tend to forge ahead according to their personal feelings.

Since we had no precedent for such an occasion, we had to improvise. We found a little box and gently deposited our beloved canary into it. After some discussion, we wended our way to Van Cortlandt Park, which was near our home in Yonkers, New York. We soon faced a lovely little hill, which we climbed and proceeded to dig a small hole into which we lowered the bird. My latent rabbinic instincts began to assert themselves. What should we do next? A eulogy or prayer seemed uncalled for, so we devised an alternate plan. Near the new grave lay a medium sized rock. With a sharp utensil, we chiseled the name "Moritz" on its surface. I don't remember if we wrote the date.

I have not been back to that area for many years. Sometimes I wonder if I do happen to find myself there one day, would I attempt to retrace my steps and try to locate that little hill? And if I did, would the engraving on that rock still be legible?

It was a meaningful experience for two young boys and, in a manner of speaking, it was my first funeral.

The Demise of the Family Doctor

After arriving in the United States from Germany where he was a cardiac specialist, my father successfully passed all the required examinations to become a doctor in America. With the responsibilities of a family, he decided to enter the larger field of a general practitioner. As a child, it was always a treat for me to accompany my father on his home visits. Before we got into the car with a list of addresses, he would fetch his little black satchel which contained the mysterious instruments he employed during these visits.

The remunerations for a doctor at that time would be hard for someone to believe today. If memory serves me correctly, the rates were three dollars for an office appointment and five dollars for a visit to the patient's home! Of course, it must be remembered that the power of the dollar in the early 1940's was much stronger than it is today.

The differences in the role of the family doctor and the healer of today extend well beyond the salaries. The position the doctor played in the life of the family then when contrasted to the fragmented medical services being administered to the patient today are nothing less than monumental. In days of yore, the family doctor was integrally involved with the family members. More than simply addressing the currents ills, he invariably became an advisor, friend and consultant to all concerned. Prior to his arrival, the rooms had to be cleaned and tidied and he was greeted in the most respectful and cordial manner.

Similarly, prior to the Industrial Revolution, the artisan took great pride in the work of his hands. If he crafted a shoe, table or chair, it was his personal and unique creation. He took great care in its construction and much satisfaction in its completion. This all disappeared with the Industrial Revolution which introduced the conveyor belt upon which different stages of production were brought together to produce the final result. For example, one procedure was to cut the leather for a belt, another involved piercing the material with a specific number of holes, while the final stage consisted of attaching a buckle. There was little pride felt by any individual, each of whom merely pushed the button to make the machinery move the belt around the various processes.

So, too, went the fate of the family doctor. Every aspect of the healing process became departmentalized. Home calls were replaced by the patient visiting the doctor's office or being admitted to an emergency room or hospital. Granted there remained a primary care doctor, but more often than not, this was a procedural matter whereby the primary doctor directed the patient to the needed specialty procedures.

My experiences during these changes were most interesting. Being a rabbi in a comparatively small community, I hardly ever saw the inside of a waiting room. When I arrived, I was instantly taken to a side room where any pre-examination procedures were conducted. The doctor appeared shortly after and, within the shortest time, I found myself back on the street.

The apex of my rabbinical status took place while I was a rabbi in New Bedford, Massachusetts. As luck would have it, my doctor was also the president of my congregation. But that was only the beginning. He was also the owner of a hospital where I went for my check-ups. Needless to state, I again did not find myself in a waiting room. But there was another major caveat. Following my examination, the doctor would escort me into the hospital dining room, where he had an assortment of kosher TV trays and I was treated to a delicious lunch and interesting conversation. Could Blue Cross/Blue Shield offer anything comparable to such luxury?

But it was not to last. By the time I arrived in Fall River, Massachusetts, matters had drastically changed. Although my new doctor was extremely friendly to me - I even officiated at the wedding of his daughter - the days of skipping the waiting room were over. The doctor's suite took up a small amount of space on a floor with many other offices. It was a difficult transition for me. More than an hour could easily pass between the time I arrived and the time I was actually called into the doctor's office.

I fear that by now I have been forced to join the masses. An appointment must be made well in advance and I am systematically dealt with for the preliminary procedures as I am whisked into the doctor's office and objectively treated for whatever reason I came. It would seem that the position of the clergy has taken quite a turn. Suddenly we have each become just another patient. Perhaps this is a stride toward democracy.

All in all, however, I try not to view this as a bad development. Conditions change and if a person wants to stay happy, he must cheerfully "go with the flow." In fact, the present system may even have some advantages over the old one. There is a high degree of efficiency which clearly works to the benefit of the patient. Progress has been made in the time span between the patient's arrival and his meeting with the doctor. Every detail is recorded in the computer and appointments are made far in advance, enabling one to plan accordingly. On a personal level, I can truly say that all the doctors with whom I have recently had dealings have been extremely friendly and have taken a very personal interest in me.

The loss of the family doctor of yore, however, does leave a void in the structure of the family. It is certainly not a fatal omission, but the absence of this confidante and friend is to be pitied. The family physician was once considered a person whose importance far exceeded that of a medical functionary. But alas time marches on and doctors who have the time and desire to take a personal interest in their patients are few and far between. Still, I have been privileged to meet such doctors who remind me of the family healers of past years, certainly compensating for any lack in the system.

As for me, I am happy to peruse a magazine or play a computer game of chess in the waiting room as I wait for my name to be called.

On Ancestry

I have fond memories of my younger years and about family members and events which I have always remembered. Two warm and meaningful tales of these pertain to ancestors of mine whose identities I was never able to determine.

The first is of a scholar who was perennially absorbed in Talmud study. Whenever a woman entered the room, he would close the book until she left. Apparently he felt that the texts that he was studying were not meant for her eyes.

Today, such an attitude would undoubtedly be met with strong protests, although I suspect that these sentiments might still be acceptable in some parts of the ultra-Orthodox world. This scholar, who might have been my great-great grandfather, was probably a wonderful and gentle man who loved his wife and daughters, but was a product of his time. In those days, speculative Talmudic studies were solely in the realm of the menfolk. The women studied those laws which pertained to their personal lives and, of course, were proficient in prayer and the recitation of the Psalms. Nevertheless, their influence upon the family and even their husbands was powerful.

The other ancestor whose tale was always a delight to me was a man who never left home without his *Chumash* (Bible). He developed a condition wherein his hip bone protruded from his waist to a point that an immediate operation was indicated. This was still during the "horse and buggy" period and the horse-drawn ambulance pulled up in front of his home. He prepared to lie down on the stretcher, but first went to the bookshelf to extract his *Chumash.* The book was on a high shelf and, as he extended his arm to take it down, the hip bone snapped back into its proper place. He was examined and declared perfectly healthy as the ambulance left without him.

Was I Baptized?

The English love their children and cats. I mention this fact because my family and I made our way to America via England where we lived for about a year, right before WWII as the country was preparing for war. Scores of balloons tied to thick ropes dotted the sky over Finsbury Park where we lived. They were intended to trap German planes midair and bring them down. Constant air raid drills were preceded by sirens which propelled people into the nearest air raid shelter.

All of which brings me back to the love and concern of the English for their children and cats. One time, as the sirens cast their ominous wails, a British lady ran among us bearing a large canister of what she defined as holy water. She generously sprinkled the water on all children within her range and on any cats which happened to be near her. As it turned out, I was in extremely close proximity to her sprays, making me the recipient of a generous dose of "holy" water!

Which raises the question of whether or not I was actually baptized.

Quite frankly, I doubt very much that this well-meaning lady succeeded in bestowing any such benefits on me. I do believe she was making a sincere effort to protect me. Nevertheless, I have never listed this incident among my accomplishments on my curriculum vitae in seeking a rabbinical position.

Countdown for Cheesecake

The holiday of Shavuot is the culmination of a forty-nine day count from the second day of Passover until the advent of this festival. It is the generally accepted custom that dairy menus are prepared for this holiday. The reason given is that when the Children of Israel arrived at Mount Sinai, they were not acquainted with all the rules and specifics regarding the *kashrut* of meat and the mixing of milk and meat. As a result, goes the reasoning, they restricted themselves to dairy meals until after the Torah was revealed, at which time they would have all the necessary information.

This arrangement is the cause of problems among some. There are those who maintain that the Jewish festivals should be honored by partaking of meat and wine at each meal. On the other hand, they do not wish to turn their backs upon the custom which may be of importance. What to do? Many will have a small dairy meal, wait a period of time, and then have a more formal holiday repast, featuring wine and meat. Others simply do away with meat meals and only serve dairy menus. These latter meals invariably feature cheesecake, which has become a symbol of this holiday.

To me, as a young boy, these differences of opinion were non-existent. My only focus was on the delicious cheesecake which I eagerly anticipated. But it came with a price. As mentioned previously, Shavuot comes at the end of seven weeks of counting the *Omer*. Each night, a blessing is recited, followed by the day and the week as Shavuot comes closer. The challenge to us children was that if we did not forget a single night of this countdown, we were eligible to partake of the luscious mounds of cheesecake in all flavors, garnished with fruits and even ice cream.

The first days were the most difficult as is the initiation of any new habit. Reminders were placed on the bed and other places to keep us aware of the count. It was truly an annual trial of marathon proportions.

At this point, I do not remember the years in which I may have forgotten or those in which the count was complete. But I do suspect that, even if we skipped a day or two, we could always expect a generous helping of cheesecake on our plates.

I Only Eat at Home

As a child, it is always wonderful to listen to stories told by parents about events that transpired prior to one's birth. I am happy to have received my share of those tales and one stands out in my mind. My mother married into a very religious family. Her new father-in-law, Dr. Magnus Weinberg, was a rabbi and a historian. His wife, Judith, was the granddaughter of the famous Wurzburger Rav, Rabbi Seligmann Baer Bamberger (1807-1878). Shortly after her marriage, my mother was visited by (I believe) the daughter of the Wurzburger Rav. The intent of the visit was to determine if my mother had complied with all the laws of *kashrut* in her kitchen.

My mother was perfectly agreeable to show the kitchen to her visitor. After a thorough inspection, she was told, "My dear, your kitchen conforms to every iota of what is expected of a kosher home. In fact, you have a *pareve* (neither dairy nor meat) set which I don't even have in my home."

Quite happily, my mother responded, "That being the case, may I invite you to join me for lunch?"

"No, my daughter," was the reply. "You see, I only eat from my own kitchen."

It is most important to understand that there was absolutely no intent to be holier-than-thou in this response. It was a simple statement of fact. There may be such folks today, although I have not run into them. These people were very pious and sincerely felt that the religious standards of others may not conform to their own or that others may not be as scrupulous. As a result, they quietly relied only on themselves. As long as they did not flaunt their observance, I have a deep respect for their consistency.

Today, there are so many levels of *kashrut*, each one stricter than the next. Many people only trust certain establishments and will not eat in others. On airplanes which advertise all their food as being carefully supervised, there are passengers who insist on being served a "higher degree" of kosher.

The truth of the matter is that while everyone's intent may be the very best, the rules of chance dictate that error is inevitable in the area of mass food production.

So if anyone seeks the closest to perfection, instead of praising himself at which restaurant he eats, he should conform to my great-grandmother's dictum, "I only eat at home."

THE CYCLE OF LIFE

Everything has its season and there is a time for everything under the heaven. A time to be born and a time to die...a time to weep and a time to laugh...a time to mourn and a time to dance...a time for peace and a time for war.
(Ecclesiastes 3:1-8)

A Time for all Occasions

The book of Kings describes the fascinating story of how King Solomon achieved the great wisdom for which he was famous. When he was a young man, God appeared to him in a dream and offered him the fulfillment of one wish. All Solomon asked for was wisdom so that he could better judge his people. This request pleased God so much that not only did He grant him his wish, but He also bestowed upon him riches and honor. Tradition states that Solomon wrote three major books which have remained the epitome of the deepest insights and knowledge throughout the generations.

Ecclesiastes (*Kohelet*) is the book which he wrote in the latter part of his life. At the beginning of the third chapter, he lists various periods in a person's life:

> Everything has its season and there is a time for everything under the heaven. A time to be born and a time to die; a time to weep and a time to laugh; a time to cry and a time to dance; a time for peace and a time for war.

This section has always left me somewhat puzzled. When compared to the deep wisdom expressed in all the other parts of the book, these verses seem to pale in their simplicity. We are all quite aware of the fact that one is born and one dies. Do we need to be told that laughing is to be expected at a happy occasion? Would we presume people laugh at a funeral? It seems strange that the wisest of men should present us with facts that are so apparent that they speak for themselves.

Upon giving the matter due consideration, a great truth dawned upon me. King Solomon was not telling us what the existential reality is, but rather how we should relate to it. For example, man should be aware of his mortality and act accordingly. The time of death is hidden from us and therefore, we should always be prepared.

There are those who, for unworthy reasons, begrudge the bride and groom the happiness to which they are entitled. Others may have various misgivings at a wedding. They cannot get themselves to laugh and be happy. Such people should overcome their reservations and realize that it is a time of joy and become part of it. No matter how great the *simcha* (joyous occasion), there are always some with long faces and woes. Solomon advises them to mend their ways.

History has always been burdened with those who refused to recognize lurking danger and would try to appease dictators with murderous agendas. *Kohelet* teaches that, sad as it may be, there is a time for war when battle must be waged against an implacable enemy. Failure to engage in warfare at such a crucial time could result in even more dire consequences in the future. Conversely, there are times when war can possibly be avoided and further avenues of peace should be explored.

In short, King Solomon's sage advice to all of us is to seriously and realistically assess the situation in which we find ourselves at any given moment. By so doing, we can act in a reasonable manner and successfully plan ahead in the pursuit of our desired goals.

Solomon's words may seem somewhat simplistic on the surface, but the truth of their wisdom is of infinite depth.

Nothing New

Over the past few decades, child psychologists have been constantly in the spotlight espousing their new-found discoveries concerning the strong influence of past experiences on infants, no matter how young.

This was hardly news to the Jewish people. Already dating back to tales from the Talmud, we find mothers wheeling their baby carriages through Jewish study halls so that their infants could hear and absorb the sounds of study among Torah scholars.

Perhaps the most delightful incident on this subject is found in the Mishna in Tractate *Sukka* (Chapter 2, Mishna 8). We read that Shammai's daughter-in-law gave birth to a baby boy. When the festival of Sukkot arrived, this great and elderly sage made a hole in the ceiling over the baby's bed and covered it with *schach* (temporary ceiling of a Sukka).

Certainly this new-born baby was not yet required to live in a Sukka, yet it seems that Shammai was acting with a definite purpose. He apparently understood that the very first impressions of an infant become the primary sources for lifetime. Knowing this, Shammai arranged for the little baby to lie under the *schach* in the Sukka soon after its birth.

The Mishna does not relate the sequel to this incident. I refer to what must have transpired when Shammai's daughter-in-law entered the bedroom and saw that he had carved a hole in the bedroom ceiling!

No Tallit Until Marriage

When a boy reaches the age of bar mitzva, the family decides whether or not he will immediately begin to wear a *tallit* (prayer shawl) or wait until his marriage. Following the German Jewish *minhag*, my family's custom has always been that the boy begins to wear his *tallit* as soon as he becomes a bar mitzva. This, however, is not the prevalent custom. It would seem that the majority waits until marriage. It is a decision with which I respectfully disagree. I have seen men even in advanced age who don their *tefillin* (phylacteries), but not a *tallit*, because they are not married.

The predominant rationale for this delay is the proximity in the Torah between the verse: "You shall make fringes for yourself" (Deuteronomy 22:12) and the verse: "When a man takes a woman (in marriage)" (Deuteronomy 22:13). This juxtaposition is interpreted to demonstrate that the use of *tallit* is concurrent with marriage.

I have also heard an opinion that by beginning to don a *tallit* at the time of marriage, the groom is placing himself into a higher spiritual dimension.

However, as I stated previously, none of these theories or speculations satisfied me and it always seemed to me that this is a custom which somehow got started, followed by attempts to justify it.

But I would ask myself, "Who am I?" If there are great rabbis who instruct their sons to refrain from wearing a *tallit* until they stand under the *chuppa* (marriage canopy), then I should not be critical.

And so it was with a great deal of contentment that I discovered the following quote in the *Mishna Berura* of the *Chofetz Chaim* (Rabbi Yisrael Meir Kagan – 1838-1933):

"To train him" – All these (regulations) are only valid before he reaches the age of thirteen, but from the age of thirteen and onward, he is obligated to wear *tzitzit* just like an adult. And what is written in the teachings of the Maharil in the laws of marriage that there is a custom that also older boys (young men) do not wrap themselves in *tzitzit* (a *tallit*) and rely (for this custom) upon the verse, "You shall make *tzitzit* for yourself" and the neighboring verse, "When a man takes a woman" – **this is a surprising thing, since it means that until he marries, he sits and neglects the commandment of *tzitzit*."** (*Mishna Brura*, Laws of *Tzitzit*, *Siman* 17, Note 10)

Thus, while it is certainly not my intention to disparage the many men who do not wear a *tallit* until they are married (and some never get married!), it is a custom for which I simply cannot find any merit and find myself very vindicated by the support of no lesser a sage than the *Chofetz Chaim*.

Feting the Bride and Groom

The period of mourning for the students of Rabbi Akiva who died in a plague fluctuates according to different customs. The thirty-three days are observed between Passover and Shavuot at differing intervals.

The case is related of a wedding invitation sent by a family that had concluded their period of mourning. However, the recipients of this invitation were still within their thirty-three days of mourning. Not knowing what to do, they consulted with Rabbi Moshe Feinstein.

"Leave your mourning, accept the invitation and perform the *mitzva* (commandment) of bringing joy to the bride and groom," was his reply.

It is quite clear from this response that bringing joy to a bride and groom is an imperative of great importance.

Which leads to the question of what is the essence of this *mitzva?* I believe that there is an anatomy to every commandment which we are asked to observe. Visiting the sick, for example, bids us to give moral support to the patient, finding what we can do for him and praying for him. When giving *tzedaka* (charity), it should be done in an amount that will truly help the recipient and in a manner that does not cause him any shame. And so it is with all the other commandments.

In the case of the bride and groom, it would seem that they are quite happy at having found each other. In fact, one might actually suspect that their joy would be increased if we stopped dancing around them, pumping their hands, hugging them and saturating them with shouts of good wishes.

Where, then, lies the essence of this *mitzva* which we are clearly obligated to observe? What are we contributing to the new couple that they may be missing?

Shortly after I was married, my mother shared an astounding fact with me. My father actually shed a few tears after I had moved away to my new home with my wife. He certainly was not sorry that I had married. It was simply a human reaction to the loss he was feeling after I had been a regular member of my home for over two decades. This had now radically and permanently changed.

So the Torah tells us, "Therefore a man shall leave his father and his mother and cling to his wife and they shall become one flesh" (Genesis 2:24).

But that is not all. King Solomon tells us, "A generation goes and a generation comes" (Ecclesiastes 1:4). Through their marriage, the bride and groom are making their parents prospective grandparents and their grandparents potential great-grandparents. In short, they are moving each generation back one step.

It is certainly possible that the bride and groom may not be aware of this on a conscious level. Possibly, it is a remote thought or feeling relegated to the subconscious. Nevertheless, the emotion may have crept in which caused them to sense some subtle sorrow, thereby reducing their joy in an ever so slightly manner.

It is here that the *mitzva* asserts itself. In a loud and clear way, we assure the new couple, again and again, that our joy is without the slightest reservation. We look with pride and delight at their establishing a new home. Our moving into a different generation because of the arrival of beloved new infants is nothing but a source of our deepest happiness.

That, I believe, is the essence of the commandment to bring ever more joy to the bride and groom. It is not enough for us to feel this joy; it is our responsibility to convey it to them.

Dancing to the Chuppa

What I consider an amazing part of a Mishna at the end of Tractate *Taanit* (4:8), reads as follows:

> There were no (more joyous) holidays for Israel than the fifteenth of Av and Yom Kippur, for on them the daughters of Jerusalem would go forth in borrowed white garments … and dance in the vineyards. And what did they say? "Young man, lift up your eyes and see who to choose for yourself."

It was a time of great joy. The dancing girls would all wear simple white dresses borrowed from each other and the men would possibly choose a bride from among them. Apparently, many matches were made on those two annual happy occasions.

Now let us fast-forward to our own day. A strictly Orthodox girls' Yeshiva announces that in a certain adjacent park, the students of the graduating class will dance to accompanying *klezmer* music on the forthcoming fifteenth of Av. All Yeshiva boys are invited to attend and, if so inclined, they are welcome to propose marriage to one of the dancers.

It would seem to me that if this would be announced in any country today, including Israel, heavy contingents of riot police would have to be summoned on an emergency basis to deal with the mass of frenzied demonstrations that would descend against those hapless dancers and observers that were doing nothing more than replicating what transpired in the days of the Talmud.

It was Rabban Shimon ben Gamliel who reported that this is exactly what happened on the fifteenth of Av and on Yom Kippur.

I cannot help but wonder what happened along the way.

No Mirrors at Shiva

T he observance of *Shiva,* the seven days immediately following the interment of a close relative, is replete with laws and customs designed to honor the deceased and afford a measure of comfort to the bereaved. Logical explanations are offered for most of these customs. It is understandable why mourners should remain at home during this period, sit on low stools and refrain from other activities which may be contrary to the sadness which is expressed during this period.

One of the customs, however, whose origins and reasons are not quite as clear is the covering of all the mirrors in the mourners' home from the time they arrive after the funeral until the end of the seven-day period.

One of the explanations for this custom which I have heard is a practical one. During the initial and intense sorrow, little attention is paid to personal appearance. It is prohibited for men to shave during this period. If the mirrors were uncovered and available for viewing, it could be an actual shock for the mourner to see him/herself in this deteriorated state. It could also be a source of embarrassment since visitors are constantly arriving. The covered mirrors do away with any of these concerns.

The other explanation is more on the spiritual side. The covered mirrors are both a statement and a lesson. There is nothing more fickle than a mirror. As long as the person stands in front of it, the reflection of that individual is strong and clear. As soon as the person steps away, however, the image disappears as if it had never been there. It is entirely "forgotten."

By covering the mirror, we are stating that even though the physical person is no longer with us, the spiritual presence will remain as strong as it was during his/her lifetime. As the intensity of mourning lessens, memory will last forever.

While I do not have any proof of the actual reason for mirrors to be covered in a *Shiva* home, this latter reason has always greatly appealed to me. There is a great deal of truth in it. Memory and respect of departed close relatives is an important halachic imperative and gives greater meaning to our own lives.

Of Pebbles and Boulders

A generally accepted custom upon visiting a cemetery is to place a small stone or pebble upon the headstone of the grave being visited. While there are varied mystical and kabbalistic reasons for this custom, there is one very practical explanation. It is a simple and thoughtful way of displaying that a loved one has been remembered by a visitor and is a mark of respect to the person who died.

Quite some time ago, I began to notice an unbelievable phenomenon. Many of the little stones that had graced the monuments over the graves had been replaced by stones of huge sizes, almost boulders. This new practice struck me as seriously objectionable. One of the main messages of our faith is that in death, there is equality. It is for this reason that traditional Jewish people bury their deceased in plain white garments. Most cemeteries allow only modest headstones to mark the graves.

In direct contrast to this principle, some people have recently chosen to drag huge rocks onto the headstones. While I do not question the fact that they are doing it as a sign of love for a dear one who has passed away, they could not be more misguided.

My father had a wonderful sense of humor and I am sure that if he could, he would have said, "Please get that rock off my headstone; it is giving me a headache!"

One View of Hell

After having lived a good life, a man came to the afterlife. He was first shown a view of heaven, where he saw people sitting around tables engaged in the intensive study of books pertaining to the Bible and the Talmud.

Not having been much of a scholar, he asked to be shown an overview of Hell, although he made it clear that his request was just out of a general interest.

In compliance with his wishes, he was escorted into a huge banquet hall. Long tables were laden with the most delicious foods he had ever seen. Meats and vegetables of all types were heaped in abundance. There were exotic fruits and delectable cakes of every description.

Yet, something seemed wrong. The people sitting around the tables were pale, listless and seemed on the verge of starvation as they stared longingly at the food in front of them.

"What is wrong with all those people?" the visitor asked. "They look starved. Why aren't they eating all that delicious food?"

"If you will look closely at the silverware," his escort responded, "you will note that the forks and spoons are very long. There is no way that they can feed themselves with those long utensils."

The man thought about that a moment before commenting. "But there is such a simple solution. All they have to do is extend their forks to their neighbors and feed each other."

The escort smiled. "They would rather starve."

And that, my friends, is Hell.

Kaddish on Festivals

It is axiomatic in Halacha (Jewish law) that the joy of celebrating the Jewish holidays cannot coincide with mourning for close relatives. If one were to absorb these two conflicting emotions simultaneously, it would be an exercise in schizophrenia; it could not be done. Always sensitive to human nature, the Halacha teaches that all public manifestations of mourning, including *Shiva,* must cease with the onset of the festival.

Shabbat is treated somewhat differently. The overriding emotion of this day, unlike the joy of festivals, is *oneg,* which, loosely translated, means "pleasure." Pleasure and mourning are not considered mutually exclusive, as a result of which, Shabbat is counted as one of the seven days of *Shiva,* although any external manifestations of mourning must be concealed.

Which, in my opinion, creates a basic question. There are a number of *Kaddish* categories during religious services. One of them is the Mourners' *Kaddish,* to be recited for parents during the eleven-month period following their death. Now it would seem to me that there is no greater public expression of sadness and mourning than this recitation both on Shabbat, as well as on festivals. Yet, it is done without reservation in all synagogues. I have never attended a synagogue which does not allow the Mourners' *Kaddish* on Shabbat or festivals.

How can this be?

Claiming that death is not mentioned in the *Kaddish* strikes me as a very unsatisfactory response. The entire congregation clearly sees and is cognizant of the fact that only the mourners are offering this recitation in observance of their loss and out of love and respect for the departed.

The actual expression of death in the prayer seems almost irrelevant in reference to this issue.

The same question can be asked regarding *Yizkor* (memorial service) on the last days of the festivals. It is clearly a service to commemorate those who have passed on. In fact, the *Kayl Malei* memorial prayer is chanted as part of that service. This is a prayer which is never permitted at any other time on holidays and usually only on Shabbat. Asserting that the memorial prayer is named *Yizkor,* which means to "remember," as opposed to "mourn," again is a weak response. The prayers evoke great sadness. I remember when I was younger and people were more demonstrative, that loud wailing would emanate from the women's section and many a silent tear was shed by others during the recitation of *Yizkor.*

While I have not made a study of the history of *Kaddish* and *Yizkor,* I have a theory which accounts for the admission of these prayers into our Shabbat and Yom Tov liturgies. Throughout our Halachic works, there is a rule that laws may not be promulgated that the people cannot (or will not) accept. The intensity of the love and memory for parents and close relatives is a well-known fact among the Jewish people. It would be reasonable to assume that if *Kaddish* would only be permitted to be recited on weekdays, but forbidden on Shabbat and festivals, it would probably have been recited quietly by the mourners. Religious legislation which would have sought to curtail this emotional declaration on these days would not have succeeded.

The Fifth Commandment is powerfully observed and transcends death. Love and respect for parents remain with children throughout their lives. No wonder then that *Kaddish* and *Yizkor* are part of our holy days. There is no way that they could have been excluded.

THE JEWISH CALENDAR

What kind of a summer does a Jew have? Seven weeks he counts (the Omer), three weeks (before Tisha B'Av) he cries and four weeks he blows (the Shofar) - and the summer is over. (Dr. Seligmann Weinberg, my father)

The Most Important Month of the Year

Rabbi Samson Raphael Hirsch (1808-1888) described the Jewish holidays as being the luminaries that light up the otherwise dark road of the weeks and months. Well in advance of the impending festival, it already casts its rays. The light gets stronger until everyone revels in its unique splendor. Even after it has passed, the afterglow of the festival remains for some time.

Consider the Hebrew month of Adar. The joyful festival of Purim springs to mind. I am sure there is no dearth of people who would choose this month as their favorite. Costumes, parties, exchanging food gifts, and far from the least attraction - the Purim banquet - all add to the joy of the holiday.

On a more spiritual plane is the festival of Chanuka, with its beautiful eight-pronged Menorah, celebrated in the month of Kislev. Family gatherings with *sufganiyot* (doughnuts), potato latkes and the spinning dreidels go far to make this month a favorite.

The month probably voted as favorite by the majority is Nisan with its illustrious centerpiece of Passover and the *Seder*, the great holiday of freedom, shining its beacon to family and friends.

So it goes with the other months. Some festivals are more prominent than others, but everyone can choose the month with the holiday which he/she likes best.

You are no doubt wondering which month I consider the most important. Before divulging this information, let me apprise you of the fact that there is one month in the Jewish calendar which cannot claim even a single Jewish festival, not even a fast day!

The month to which I refer is Cheshvan, also called Mar-Cheshvan. Among other meanings, *"mar"* can be translated as "bitter." Some maintain that because this month is bereft of any festival whatsoever, it is experienced with an element of bitterness.

That having been said, my choice of Cheshvan as the most important month should come as somewhat of a surprise. But please understand. I love each and every one of the holidays. Each has a special and unique message and I revel in their observance.

So let me explain why Cheshvan is so welcome and so vital to me.

Cheshvan arrives directly after the month of Tishrei which is virtually bursting with holidays. Tishrei starts with Rosh Hashana, the New Year, continues with Yom Kippur, the sacred Day of Atonement, and just days later, the joyous festivals of Sukkot and Simchat Torah.

The routine and quiet which follow this turbulent month is calming and most appreciated. Herein, I feel, lies the true strength and meaning of the Jewish calendar. Man cannot live on the crest. Celebrations are welcome and laden with joy if they come at intervals. However, routine must be the main goal which gives the basic meaning to our daily lives.

And so, after the tumult of a kaleidoscope of somber and joyous holidays in the month of Tishrei, we greet a month that has no holidays whatsoever. This is our opportunity to carry out the resolutions we made during the month of Tishrei. It is the time to harness the spiritual ecstasies we experienced during the High Holiday period into meaningful daily activities.

And that is the reason why, although I treasure every month and holiday, the month that I deem to be the most important in the overall picture is Cheshvan which affords me the opportunity to carry out the beautiful and inspirational routines that center around the Torah and the age hallowed traditions of Judaism.

The Power of Leadership

There is a compelling question which presents itself when examining the Jewish calendar. We find days and periods which are marked and observed annually and there are other similar events which are given hardly any distinction at all.

I refer, for example, to the festival of Purim. The deliverance of the Persian Jewish community from the evil Haman was unquestionably a great miracle and event. We observe it meticulously. There is the previous day of the Fast of Esther on which all Jews are expected to refrain from food and drink. Special commandments are observed on the day of Purim as we listen to the *Megilla* (Scroll of Esther), accompanied by other customs and ceremonies. Even the day following the holiday, Shushan Purim, is a semi-festival which is especially significant in cities which were walled since the time of Joshua.

On the other end of the spectrum, we have the seven-week period of *Sefirat Ha'Omer* (Counting of the *Omer*). I do not refer to the count between Passover and Shavuot. That was mandated by the Torah and has an unequivocal basis. I refer to the semi-mourning which is observed for thirty-three days during this period of seven weeks. The reason for this observance is the commemoration of the death of 24,000 students of Rabbi Akiva. Certainly this was a tragedy of the greatest magnitude. It can further be argued that this period of mourning is not only to commemorate the loss of life of all these students. Rather, the loss of Torah scholarship was very great, for they were all sages in their own right.

But the question remains. Is not our history replete with terrible losses through persecution and untold calamities? Were not many of the victims great Torah scholars? Is there a dearth of plagues, pogroms and other tragedies which befell our people throughout the years, taking with them some of the greatest Torah luminaries in our history? How is it, then, that a lengthy period of semi-mourning was instituted specifically for the students of Rabbi Akiva to the apparent exclusion of many others?

One possible answer lies in the religious leadership which was prevalent at the time of each event.

The clear and uncontested religious authority at the time of Purim was Mordechai. Not only did he exert great influence over Esther, even when she reigned as queen, but he instituted all aspects of Purim in an official and authorized manner. The *Megilla* points out in great detail how his generation accepted all his edicts and we know that succeeding generations also followed his directives.

The mourning period for the students of Rabbi Akiva became universally accepted for the same reason. Rabbi Akiva loomed as one of the greatest and undisputed sages of his day. The loss of so many thousands of his students marked the event as a historic tragedy to be observed not only in his own day, but for all time. It can safely be assumed that Rabbi Akiva ordered this period of mourning which was accepted and continued through the generations.

Such is the nature of greatness. It has the power to influence both the contemporary generation, as well as future ones. Its opposite is mediocrity. When Torah leadership lacks the moral strength and authority to lead, it becomes very difficult to establish events in their proper historic context.

This lack of communal influence and control is very apparent in our own day in which two of the most traumatic and historically significant events have transpired. There is very little unanimity as to how a day commemorating the *Shoah* (Holocaust) should be observed. Generally, the day marking the outbreak of the Warsaw ghetto uprising is designated for programs and remembrance. Since there is no religious leadership even remotely on par with Mordechai or Rabbi Akiva, the contemporary observances cannot compare with the traditions established in those days.

The same holds true of *Yom Ha'atzmaut* - Israel Independence Day and Yom Yerushalayim – Jerusalem Day. There is constant disagreement about whether or not the Hallel prayer should be recited in its entirety, in its abridged form, or not at all. Should the blessings for Hallel be recited?

It is very disconcerting to look into many a *Luach* (calendar) and note that these days are not even listed.

In the State of Israel today, somehow these crucial and defining days have begun to take on a life of their own. For example, a siren is sounded for one or two minutes on the day commemorating the *Shoah* and on *Yom Hazikaron,* the day preceding Israel's Independence Day, when everyone is expected to stand in silent respect and reverence. There is a small minority who disregard these moments and go about their business as usual. However, the custom continues, gaining strength from year to year. There is an order of prayers included in many Israeli prayer books and signs are becoming apparent that these days will find a lasting place in our future calendar.

Sad to note, however, religious leadership is woefully divided and very intimidated by each other. The love which was so strong among Torah scholars, for example between Hillel and Shammai, is far from apparent today. If one religious leader makes a decision, one can almost expect severe criticism and condemnation to follow from other religious denominations. One can only hope that this fractious behavior will change. In the meantime, despite a lack of strong religious leadership, the people of Israel and the spirit that manifests itself in that blessed country and society prevails.

The emerging Israel is becoming the reflection of the verse, "Out of Zion shall go forth the Torah and the word of God from Jerusalem" (Isaiah 2:3).

Why is This Passover Different?

There are years when the first day of Passover coincides with Shabbat. When this occurs, there are a number of unique aspects to this combination. One of them raises a most interesting question. When the first day of Rosh Hashana coincides with Shabbat, the *shofar* is not sounded because of the danger that the Sabbath may be violated by someone carrying the *shofar* into the public domain. As a result, the *shofar* is sounded only on the second day of Rosh Hashana.

The same holds true for the festival of Sukkot. If the first day of Sukkot coincides with Shabbat, the *lulav* is not taken until the second day. Again, this is done to protect the Shabbat from being violated.

Which brings up the question of the *matza*. When the first day of Passover corresponds with Shabbat, why is the *mitzva* of eating the *matza* not postponed until the second night as is the case in the previous two instances? After all, if a person left his *matza* in a distant place where it was protected until the holiday and then forgot to bring it into his house before Shabbat, would there not be a similar danger that he may violate Shabbat?

My solution to the problem is that *matza* is really an extension of *lechem mishne* (two loaves of bread), which are placed on the table every Friday afternoon prior to Shabbat. It is most unlikely that a person would place two loaves of bread on the table right before Passover begins. In fact, at that time of the day, it is already forbidden to have *chametz* (leavened food) in one's possession. So, unlike the *shofar* and the *lulav* which occur only on an annual basis, the *matza*, in a sense, is a weekly occurrence and would be placed on the table well before Shabbat begins. In fact, *matza* can be used on Friday eves throughout the year.

I believe that there is another aspect to this solution. If the Rabbis had chosen not to allow the *matza* to be eaten on the first night of Passover which coincides with Shabbat, it would really have been to the detriment of the Sabbath. What could have been used for the *motzi* blessing? Bread would have been out of the question and the *matza* would have been postponed! Under those conditions, individual blessings would have had to be pronounced over each food eaten. Certainly this would not have been either in the spirit of Shabbat or Passover.

So, therefore, although Shabbat and Passover coincide on the first day of the festival, it is perfectly permissible to perform the *mitzva* of eating the *matza* on Friday evening in honor of both days.

Thirty-Three Days?

The forty-nine days between Passover and Shavuot forge a link between these two festivals. The Exodus from Egypt was not an end in itself, but a prelude to our receiving the Torah at Mount Sinai as celebrated by the festival of Shavuot seven weeks later. Originally, these were days of joyful anticipation as we annually relived the days and weeks which brought us ever closer to the great Revelation.

Many centuries later, in the latter part of the first century into the second century, a great tragedy occurred. Rabbi Akiva was one of the greatest rabbis of his day, with a following of thousands of students. According to historical tradition, these students acted very badly toward one another. Propelled by jealousy, they refused to share their Torah studies and exhibited baseless hatred among themselves.

During the period of the counting of the *Omer*, a plague broke out among the students, to which no less than 24,000 fell victim. The days of the happy eagerness of the *Omer* were now beclouded by this catastrophe. For a period of thirty-three days (divided differently among differing customs), a period of partial mourning was ordained. Weddings did not take place, haircuts were proscribed and public entertainment was banned.

This period of mourning, coinciding with a once happy and anticipatory era in the Jewish calendar, always struck me as being out of context. Granted that these students must have been great scholars who would have contributed significantly to Jewish knowledge ... but thirty-three days! Something simply does not compute.

What about the ten great rabbis martyred by the Romans? What days and weeks of mourning were set aside for the myriads of innocent men, women and children who were murdered *Al Kiddush Hashem* (for the sanctification of God's sake) throughout our history?

There is another element to be considered. The students of Rabbi Akiva died by God's decree. They were not murdered. In general, we are commanded to accept God's will by reciting the blessing of *Baruch Dayan Ha'emet* (blessed be the True Judge). If, for example, a person lost a very beloved parent and declared that he would extend his *Shiva* by an extra three days to demonstrate this love, he would be in serious violation of proper Jewish conduct.

This is certainly not an attempt to minimize the tragedy of the death of so many great students; it is an effort to understand why such a long period of mourning has been ordained for these scholars while no comparable memorials exist for most other persons or groups in history.

Slowly but surely the answer began to dawn upon me. Something was happening at that time which eclipsed even the catastrophic death of these scholars. Without delving into the many details occurring at this time, in the years of 132-136 C.E., Shimon Bar Kochba led a revolt against the Roman oppressors. Rabbi Akiva declared him to be the *Mashiach* (Messiah). Now it must be remembered that Rabbi Akiva was among the greatest Jewish sages of all time. If he made such a decision, it was not to be taken lightly. There is every reason to believe that Bar Kochba was actually the Messiah.

Yet, the revolt failed and the second Jewish Commonwealth came to an ignominious end. In light of Rabbi Akiva's declaring Bar Kochba as the *Mashiach,* how could this be?

The senseless and offensive hatred of Rabbi Akiva's students towards each other negated and terminated the validity and success of Bar Kochba. This was not the atmosphere in which the Messiah could flourish, as a result of which it was terminated and postponed for a future era.

Now we can understand the great length of time that has been set aside for this mourning period. Sad as the death of so many students was, it was dwarfed by the inability of the Messianic period to begin. If it had happened, perhaps there would not have been two World Wars, countless persecutions and the greatest tragedy wrought by mankind ... the Shoah.

As we count the days of the Omer, the challenge to us is clear. By removing jealousy and hatred from our lives, we can undo the mourning of this period. The counting will become one of joyful anticipation of reaching Sinai and greeting the promised *Mashiach*.

A Day of Distinction

Far be it from me to take issue with the names that our tradition ascribes to special days in the Jewish calendar. However, there is one such day, whose name is a mystery. I refer to the fourth day before the festival of Shavuot, named *Yom Hameyuchas,* the Day of Distinction.

Distinction? Consult any Jewish calendar and it is most likely that you will not find this day listed. You will come across it only in the *Luach*, which is the little booklet outlining the order of the prayers for each day.

It is clear that there had to be a reason for this name and some very weak ones may be found here and there. Let us first see the position of this day in terms of its neighbors.

Each year, the Day of Distinction is preceded by *Rosh Chodesh* (the New Moon) of the Hebrew month of Sivan. It is always followed by the three important days prior to the festival of Shavuot. So this undesignated and seemingly normal day finds itself sandwiched between two rather important calendrical landmarks.

Which brings me to an analogy. They say that there is no more offending odor than that of a tannery – the place where animal hides are turned into leather. Should a person pass through such an area or spend some time there, even if only for a short time, he will leave the tannery with a residual repulsive smell that will leave him isolated from human contact.

Now let us look at the other side of the equation. If a person finds himself in a perfumery, all he has to do is spend a little time there and he will smell like a budding rose upon exiting. People will be drawn to the wonderful aroma.

It is precisely this condition which marks our Day of Distinction.

Each year, it finds itself at the right place at the right time. *Rosh Chodesh*, the head of the month, is a minor festival and the three days preceding Shavuot are also important days.

Each and every year, our simple day finds itself sandwiched between them. And *that* is the source for its unique distinction!

There is an obvious lesson in this for us all. Perhaps we cannot always achieve great results or become famous among our peers. That is perfectly fine as long as we manage to be in the right place at the right time. This means that we should choose our friends and neighborhoods in a way that will enhance our lives. We don't always have to do; sometimes it is enough to just make the proper choice.

That is how this otherwise insignificant day came to be known as the Day of Distinction.

Should you feel that there has to be a little something extra to qualify this day for such a lofty title, consider the fact that the day of the week which marks the Day of Distinction is the same day of the week which coincides with the following Yom Kippur *(*Day of Atonement*)*.

Sadness on Rosh Chodesh?

There are twelve unique holidays in the Jewish calendar which are considered to be of a minor nature. During a Jewish leap year, there are thirteen such special days. I refer to Rosh Chodesh, the beginning of each month. Unlike the secular calendar, which only marks the passing of the year by the major festival of New Year, the beginning of each month in the Hebrew calendar begins with this minor festival. It is marked by additional prayers of a joyful nature and restrictions to mourning practices. In biblical times, these days were celebrated with banquets.

Each year, something bothers me when we reach the month of Av, ushering in a period of mourning culminating in the fast day of Tisha B'Av. The period between the first day of Av and Tisha B'Av is known as the "Nine Days." Throughout these days, there are many regulations which curtail enjoyable experiences. Except for Shabbat, we are not allowed to eat meat or drink wine. Swimming for pleasure, weddings, and other such festive activities, are also prohibited.

I fully understand and appreciate all these rules and customs which express a feeling of sadness as we approach the day on which both Holy Temples were destroyed. What I fail to understand, however, is why the day of Rosh Chodesh, which by definition and practice is a happy day, should be included as one of the days on which mourning is mandated.

I consider it almost an exercise in schizophrenia when we chant the happy Hallel songs, such as, "This is the day which the Lord has made, let us be happy and joyful in it," and then revert to the mourning restrictions. My feeling has always been that this period of sadness should begin on the day after Rosh Chodesh.

Norbert Weinberg

I do not consider this personal unsolved puzzle to be a major one. I comply with the accepted tradition of beginning the mourning period as universally practiced, but these questions gnaw at me each year as Rosh Chodesh Av approaches. I realize that this is only an Ashkenazic problem, since the Sefardim apply these restrictions solely during the week in which Tisha B'Av falls.

Perhaps some kind person, when reading about this dilemma, will have the answer and be good enough to share it with me.

How Many Fast Days?

As I write these lines, I am in Efrat, Israel, fasting in observance of *Shiva Asar B'Tammuz,* the seventeenth day of the Hebrew month of Tammuz.

I am fasting with mixed feelings. Let me explain.

There are six days of fasting each year. The four that deal with Jerusalem and the destruction of the Holy Temples are Asara B'Tevet, Shiva Asar B'Tammuz, Tzom Gedaliah, and Tisha B'Av. The fast day before the festival of Purim is Taanit Esther and the sixth fast day is Yom Kippur, the Day of Atonement.

Of all these days, I have no question as to the legitimacy and necessity of Yom Kippur, which is mandated by the Torah and is the great day of the expiation of the sins of the Jewish people at the advent of the New Year.

Tisha B'Av, the ninth day of the Hebrew month of Av, commemorates the destruction of both Holy Temples. The Third Holy Temple has not yet been built and the mourning for the destruction of the First and Second Temples blends with the hope and determination of the Jewish people to bring about the building of the Third Holy Temple.

Please do not misunderstand my following words. I have continued to fast on all six days. However, strictly as an individual, I cannot state that my feelings on Yom Kippur and Tisha B'Av are the same as on the other four fasts.

It is hard to justify the reasons for the remaining four fast days with contemporary Israeli life. It is crystal clear why the Jews of Shushan fasted during their time of crisis. What is difficult to understand is why we are fasting about that matter today. I believe that I have a possible answer.

Mordechai was a powerful leader. He successfully and brilliantly navigated the Jewish people through the crisis brought about by Haman's hatred. He gave specific instructions as to how this great deliverance should be celebrated annually for all time to come, and he was successful in doing so. What also remained was the retention of the day of fasting prior to the joyous festival of Purim. Some say that it commemorates the three days of fasting decreed by Esther, while others maintain that it recalls the day of fasting prior to the battle against the Persians. I find it somewhat difficult to understand why we would maintain an annual fast precipitated by the danger which befell the Jewish community of Persia. If we were to decree such fasts for all the threatened perils with which the Jewish people were threatened throughout the centuries, every day of the calendar would no doubt be a fast day! Again, I believe that it was because of the power and authority wielded by Mordechai that the fast day was declared for that time and for all time to follow.

I have similar reservations regarding the three "minor" fast days associated with Tisha B'Av. I am fully aware of the fact that the incidents which occurred on these days precipitated the causes which led to the destruction of both Holy Temples and the ensuing tragedies. However, it can also be argued that these pre-misfortunes have been rectified in their own way. On Shiva Asar B'Tammuz, a breach was made in the walls of Jerusalem, rendering its fall only a matter of a short time. Jerusalem is now surrounded by radar, the modern equivalent of those walls, and is protected by a powerful air force and army. Does the continuation of fasting on this day possibly ignore the miracles which have occurred in our time? Does it render the miracles of our own days irrelevant?

Asara B'Tevet commemorates the day that the siege was laid on Jerusalem by the Babylonians in 587 B.C.E. For 2,000 years, the Jewish people suffered from the effects of this attack in all the lands to which they were driven. In 1948, however, the results of this ancient attack were neutralized by the establishment of a sovereign Jewish state. In 1967, the borders of Israel were extended to include Jerusalem and much more of its ancient territory. Yet, the fast continues to be observed unabated, almost ignoring the sacrifices of the Jewish soldiers who fought and gave their lives for this miraculous achievement.

And finally, there is the Fast of Tzom Gedaliah, recalling the assassination of Gedaliah, whose murder ended Jewish autonomy following the destruction of the First Holy Temple. But on the fifth day of Iyar, 1948, Jewish autonomy was restored and universally recognized, except by the Arab countries. Nevertheless, the fast continues to be observed as if nothing has changed.

I fully realize that many arguments can be brought to bear as to why these days of mourning and fasting should continue, but I can also appreciate why nothing is transpiring and the status quo is being maintained. It is primarily because there is no Sanhedrin, or at least no Jewish legislative body which enjoys the respect of the majority of Jews. Can you imagine the result of any Jewish group attempting the formation of such a congress? I believe it would lead to bedlam and pandemonium.

That is the reason why I continue to fast on these days. I always make a point to include the tragedies which have befallen the Jewish people, thereby giving meaning to the fasts in a contemporary setting. Of course, we must remember that all our fasts are for personal repentance and improvement.

However, I am quite certain that no changes will be forthcoming regarding these fasts until that great time of the advent of the *Mashiach* (the Messiah). So in the meantime, I will continue to fast on these designated days for all the tragedies which our people have suffered coupled with the hope and prayer that the Messiah's appearance will transpire in the nearest future.

Napoleon and the Holy Temple

Although I cannot verify the authenticity of this story, its plausibility is so strong that it left an impression on me which I would like to share.

Tisha B'Av, the ninth day of the Hebrew month of Av, is the saddest day in the Jewish calendar. Among many other tragedies, both Holy Temples, although many years apart, were destroyed on this day. It was the cause of the two thousand-year exile of the Jewish people and is annually observed by fasting and many other customs of mourning.

The story to which I refer had Napoleon Bonaparte and his escorts walking along a street of Paris. Their walk took them past a synagogue whose doors, because of the heat, were wide open. The sounds of wailing and mournful chants spilled onto the streets. Napoleon stopped and asked if anyone knew the reason for this outpouring of grief.

"Your majesty," one of his advisors replied, "The Jews are mourning the destruction of their Holy Temple."

"What?" came the swift reply. "Why was I not informed of this happening?"

"Please understand," the aide continued. "This is not something which happened recently. You see, their Temple in Jerusalem was destroyed about seventeen centuries ago."

Napoleon stared in amazement. "And they are still sitting on the floor and weeping as if it happened yesterday?"

He entered the synagogue and addressed the surprised worshippers.

"I do not know all the details of this tragedy of yours. But of this I am sure. The Temple for which you and your people continue to weep so earnestly will surely be rebuilt."

While on the subject of Napoleon and the Jews, I would like to add the following.

Napoleon's life was threatened by a deadly fall off a cliff. A Jewish soldier who saw the danger, swiftly grabbed him and drew him to safety, thereby saving his life. With great appreciation, Napoleon asked the soldier to name anything he desired as a reward.

"Your majesty," the soldier began, "I am stationed in a division which is overseen by an extremely anti-Semitic sergeant. He is constantly tyrannizing me. I would be very grateful if you would transfer me to another unit."

"How small you Jews think," the emperor sighed. "Why did you not ask to be a sergeant yourself?"

A Tisha B' Av Concert

For many years, musical notes were a mystery to me. I always harbored a curiosity about how these cryptic symbols could be turned into music. An opportunity finally presented itself one day when I was offered a chance to receive piano lessons. It was a challenge and I responded with a fair degree of enthusiasm.

Since these lessons did not begin early in my life, I did not have the opportunity to begin training in my formative years as did my daughter Judy, who started as a young girl and now plays the piano as a virtual extension of herself. Nevertheless, I plodded ahead at a somewhat satisfactory level. It cannot be denied, however, that the ease and fluency of an even minimally accomplished pianist remained a very distant and fleeting goal.

Regardless of the results, I faithfully attended my lessons and enjoyed making slow progress. The Three Week period before Tisha B'Av was approaching and I was uncertain if I should suspend the piano lessons until after the fast day. After all, this is a period when any music for enjoyment is proscribed. Since my personal activities were concerned, I thought it best not to decide for myself, but to consult an objective rabbi.

"Why not let me hear you play a bit?" the rabbi asked solicitously.

I carefully went through one of the pieces with which I was most familiar and felt reasonably satisfied with my performance.

The rabbi's face seemed somewhat pained when he rendered his decision.

"You are certainly permitted to continue playing during the Three Weeks," he began. "In fact, you should even consider giving a concert on Tisha B'Av itself. The more people you could cajole into attending this concert, the greater will be the *mitzva!*"

Rabbinic Musings

If everyone likes the rabbi, he is not a rabbi.
If no one likes the rabbi, he is not a mensch.
(Rabbi Israel Salanter – 1809-1883)

Is the Rabbi a Teacher?

The title of this essay may be misleading. Of course a great part of a rabbi's agenda is to teach. However, I was somewhat challenged to make a choice before being ordained when I was a Hebrew school instructor in Yonkers, New York. It led me into a very significant meeting which I will explain. A representative of a teaching organization had come to our Hebrew school to review the teaching procedures and give a report. Following his observation of my class, he asked to speak to me.

"It seems you are planning to be a rabbi," he began. "I consider this to be extremely unfortunate. I watched your teaching methods closely and, to say the least, I was greatly impressed. You have a great relationship with the students and they are very involved with what you are sharing. Yet, alas, it appears that you will be following the road to the rabbinate instead of education and that will be a great loss."

I was, of course, greatly flattered by this information, but it did not deter me from my desire to be a rabbi. Except for a short period of interest in law, my goal was always to be a rabbi. Although my father was a doctor, his father was a rabbi. Since I was never interested in pursuing a medical career, the rabbinate was clearly and consistently my first choice. To me, it was somewhat of a family tradition.

The good thing about my meeting with the educator who wanted me to go into the teaching field was that I certainly did not feel that being a rabbi in any way excluded teaching. In some ways, I believe it enhanced it. Whether it was with children or adults, as a rabbi, I was always engaged in teaching. I believe I have a knack for drawing people into my mind set and capturing their imagination.

I always feel satisfied that I am conveying a combination of knowledge and inspiration by being a rabbi who stresses teaching. Among the greatest satisfactions I have experienced is when people approach me many years after we have had an encounter and tell me how their lives have been changed. Perhaps one of the most extreme such examples was a woman who wrote to me from an Indian ashram and told me she felt that she was Jewish. I communicated with her at length and she eventually married into a Chabad society.

There are quite a few such examples and each one proves to me that a rabbi and a teacher are quite interchangeable.

The Rabbi's Complaint

Having officiated at High Holiday services for many years, the details of my rabbinic duties were basically taken for granted and I never took the time to analyze them. In general, it was my responsibility to see to it that the congregation was moving along according to the order of the prayers and that the schedule was being maintained. However, the apex of my contribution was what is essentially known as the sermon. Many people wait for the delivery of the sermon and anticipate new and original ideas by the rabbi in order to become more informed and inspired, particularly on the High Holidays.

Living up to these expectations takes a great deal of research and preparation. This process begins long before the actual advent of the holidays.

Thus, it was an eye-opener for me, and also somewhat amusing, to recently hear a rabbi express a fascinating complaint.

Each year, the Cantor chants the exact same prayers.

The Torah reader repeats the identical Torah portion for Rosh Hashana and Yom Kippur each year.

The *Baal Toke'ah* (the one sounding the *shofar*) produces identical tones each year.

Yet, it is the duty of the rabbi, and only the rabbi, to present new and unused themes and ideas for each of the High Holiday sermons each year. Can you imagine the result, he complained, if the rabbi were to deliver the same sermon?

I must admit that I never thought of this, but I still like the challenge of my responsibility. While I can fully appreciate the fact that the prayers and *shofar* must be identical each year, I welcome the opportunity and responsibility of delving into new ideas and being the hopeful catalyst of introducing new inspiration into the congregation.

Stretching it a Bit

I am always touched by the moving stories of how Rabbi Levi Yitzchak of Berditchev (1740-1810) found a positive motive for any action of his people, even if those actions were not quite in harmony with the dictates of the Torah.

When I was serving as the rabbi in Norwich, Connecticut, I experienced such a situation in my own congregation one Friday evening. At the time, I lived about a fifteen minute walk from the synagogue. As the service progressed, a heavy rain began to pound upon the ceiling. A congregant approached me with the information that he was going to drive to my home to fetch my raincoat so that I would not get soaked on my way home. Knowing that I would not ride back with him in his car, he simply would not allow me to walk home without a coat. I finally succeeded in dissuading him from carrying out his plan. I was, nevertheless, deeply moved by the kind intention of this friend. "Master of the universe," I said to myself, "just look at Your children. Here is a man who is willing to violate Shabbat to help a fellow human being in order to observe the Commandment, 'You shall love your neighbor as yourself.'" In fact, this man lived in the house right next to me.

Well, maybe I was stretching it a bit, but that was how I felt at the time.

What Goes Around Comes Around

A while ago, a most unusual occurrence transpired which gave me a great deal of food for thought. During the *Selichot* season, I generally go to the synagogue of the Bostoner Rebbe. Arriving some time before the start of the services, I had the opportunity to listen to someone deliver a Talmud lecture. I was very impressed with this man's knowledge and his excellent delivery.

At a future date, I was urged to attend this rabbi's lecture on a Monday evening. I responded in the affirmative with a view to possibly sitting in on a few sessions. Shortly after such a visit, I received a call from someone who was unknown to me at the time, requesting that I refrain from attending any further classes because my presence, as a rabbi, was intimidating to some of the students.

I was totally taken aback by this call, primarily because I never considered myself in the least bit intimidating and was further shocked that any serious student of the Talmud would take it upon himself to prevent another person from attending a session of Torah study.

This seemingly inconsequential episode reminded me of a similar incident in the Talmud (Tractate *Berachot* 28a), which relates a dispute between Rabban Gamliel and Rabbi Yehoshua, resulting in the removal of the former from his position as head of the Sanhedrin in Yavneh.

Rabban Gamliel was very selective as to which students would be permitted to enter the study hall.

This is how the Talmud describes the episode:

That day (when Rabban Gamliel was removed from being the head of the court), they removed the doorkeeper (of the study hall). Permission was granted to all the students to come in. Prior to this event, only selected students could enter. Rabban Gamliel's edict was: "Any student whose inside is not as his outside (who is not sincere), may not enter the study hall!"

Of course, synagogues and study halls were often shut by anti-Semitic edicts, but here I experienced an example of being excluded by a fellow Jew! After due consideration, I decided not to take any action, but I was sorry that there was not an immediate protest by the students of that group. Sadly, letting things go by the wayside is generally the prevalent human response.

The person who had called me with the request not to re-appear approached me around Rosh Hashana time. He told me that he had heard that I was upset about the matter and apologized. I, of course, accepted his apology and have remained friendly with him ever since. However, I had the uneasy feeling that the situation had not really been resolved. It reminded me of someone who immersed himself in a ritual bath (*mikveh*) with an unclean insect (*sheretz*) in his hand. I felt that the class should have been informed that something wrong had occurred and that it is proper for all to participate in the studies.

Whenever situations like this arise, I believe that every effort should be made to fully resolve such offending matters. Whoever is a keen observer will notice that there are subtle or sometimes major repercussions in unresolved matters of this type.

The following example clearly illustrates this point.

Whether one agrees or disagrees, the fact is that Jacob took the birthright from his older brother, Esau, by subterfuge.

The book of Genesis relates how, some years later, Jacob was to marry his intended and beloved wife, Rachel. Yet, to his dismay, he discovered on the morning after the wedding that he had, in fact, as a result of deception, married Rachel's older sister, Leah.

Jacob was furious and confronted Laban, his father-in-law. The reply he received was nothing short of stunning. "Such is not done in our place, to give the younger before the elder" (Genesis 29:26).

So it would seem that what had "gone around" for Jacob and Esau, "came around" for Jacob and Rachel.

Many times, when something happens in my life, pleasant or otherwise, my mind scans the past to determine if I was involved in a similar previous experience. Very often, I can discover such a connection.

To me, the lesson is clear. Life is not a series of disconnected events. Rather, there is causality. A sin gives birth to another sin and a good deed (*mitzva*) leads to more good deeds. It is beyond our knowledge to know how these scenarios transpire, but they clearly happen. Therefore, we should always proceed with optimism and caution.

A Potential Pitfall

Yehoshua ben Perachya and Nitai the Arbelite received (the tradition) from them. Yehoshua ben Perachya said: "Provide a teacher for yourself, acquire a friend for yourself and judge all people according to their merit." (Ethics of the Fathers 1:6)

Much has been written about the difference between "making" a rabbi for oneself, as opposed to "acquiring" a friend. Certainly the relationship is different between the two. A rabbi/teacher must be looked up to and respected. His influence is educational and judicial in nature. A friend is on a par with his fellow. True friends share an equality in virtually all pursuits.

It is quite understandable why Yehoshua advised everyone to have the advantages of both a rabbi, as well as a friend. Certainly these two dimensions enrich life and produce great satisfaction. What does evoke some difficulty is why the third element was introduced into this context by the Mishna. What connection can there be between having the benefit of both a rabbi and a friend with judging one's fellows in a positive and meritorious manner?

This seeming lack of connection gnawed at me for some time until it occurred to me that the realization of these two goals, wonderful as they are in and of themselves, can be the cause of possibly stumbling into a nasty pitfall.

Let us examine the scenario. Someone has found a prominent and respected rabbi who has taken a personal interest in him. This relationship will certainly make him feel religiously secure. The closeness with this rabbi assures him that there will always be a response to any religious questions which may come up and that he will constantly be guided in spiritual matters.

Then this person had the good fortune to develop a warm relationship with a fine and decent friend. They enjoy each other's company, study together and never experience the feeling of loneliness. What more can one ask for? Our friend has attained social acceptance and a satisfactory degree of religious security.

I believe that it is at this point in the Mishna that Yehoshua warns of the danger of smugness. Someone who has achieved these wonderful advantages might feel that he is now in a position to take the liberty of judging others. "My rabbi is far superior – more religious than yours." He might look upon his newfound friend to be of a much higher caliber than the ones with whom his acquaintances consort.

A person with such attitudes unfortunately is not a rarity. So many of our communities are polarized with unfriendly and competing rabbis and friends. Diversity which should strengthen us can often be the cause for divisive friction and strife.

Thus we see that the sage advice offered by Yehoshua is very much in its proper context. The more success we have in Jewish learning and sociability, the more should it lead to humility. No matter how high one's status may have risen in any field of endeavor, one should always resist the impulse to look down on others. It is crucial to always judge others – if judge one must – with a favorable view.

Welcome!

I t is always more difficult to prepare for Shabbat when alone. My wife was away but left me clear instructions, among them to place all the food for dinner in the oven, turn on the heat for thirty minutes and then be sure to turn it off before leaving for Shabbat services. I was assured that if I follow these instructions, I would find a piping hot dinner waiting for me upon my return from shul.

I was careful to follow these preparations meticulously - with one exception. I forgot to turn the oven off before leaving. This "little" fact completely escaped me as I set about the unfamiliar chore of lighting the Sabbath candles.

I was greatly concerned when, upon my return, I realized my oversight. The house was already somewhat warmer than usual. What to do? The heat in the oven could accumulate to the point of causing a fire! I immediately started to canvas my non-Jewish neighbors with a view to hinting at my predicament in the hope that they would volunteer to turn the flames off. I knew I could not ask them directly, because that would make them my emissaries to do my bidding. This would render the action as if I had done it by myself, but I could certainly hint that I needed their help.

However, all this reasoning was to no avail because I simply could not find a single person who was home. I was quite dejected when I returned without a clue as to what to do. When I sat down at my table, the doorbell rang. This was unusual because I was not expecting anyone. Upon opening the door, two well-dressed men smilingly introduced themselves as representatives from Jehovah's Witnesses.

"Welcome!" I almost shouted at them, as I virtually pulled them into the room.

I suspect that that they were more than happily surprised at this enthusiastic welcome because the vast majority of doors that they faced were shut in their faces. After sitting them down and introducing myself as a rabbi, I related my predicament. They were extremely cordial and immediately turned off the oven. In fact, I believe that they were quite impressed with the fact that I was a rabbi and did not even try to convert me! We had a wonderful conversation.

I don't know if they were sent from heaven, but I could not think of a more congenial and ecumenical way in which my problem could have been solved.

A Cup of Coffee with God?

The more synagogues I am privileged to visit, the more *minhagim* (customs) I see. Some are very meaningful while others, at least in my estimation, are on the somewhat foolish side. Nevertheless, if they have meaning for their congregants and are not offensive, they certainly should be observed. I find the same to be true when it comes to personal idiosyncrasies. We all have a few - some more, some less. I apply the same rationale to individual habits as to communal ones.

Lately, however, in quite a few synagogues that I frequent, I have found a rapidly developing practice which I find to be objectionable. Congregants, after having donned their *tallit* and *tefillin,* will stroll to their seats carrying a coffee mug (or other liquid), settle down in their seats and casually sip from their container every few minutes.

Should any of these folks suffer from an ailment which requires a constant intake of liquids, I would fully appreciate their doing this and would encourage them not to neglect it. However, I believe that this is far from the case. Knowing many of them, it is my firm conviction that they are doing this simply because it is enjoyable. It gives them a physical boost. Of course, they might protest that they have a tendency toward a dry throat or some such symptom, but in no way does it justify sipping coffee while one is supposed to be in deep concentration and earnest supplication with the Almighty. The services are of comparatively short duration. Can't we pay attention to our spiritual needs and do without physical gratification for less than an hour?

Since I do not believe that these people, whose numbers are growing, are in direct conflict with any specific halachic directives, I have remained silent. However, I am quietly offended by this spectacle which, to my way of thinking, flies into the face of what any meaningful form of prayer should be.

When we attempt to have our souls come into communication with the divine, it should mean a great deal more than having a cup of coffee with God.

A Movable Synagogue

I believe that there are two aspects to the term "Wandering Jew." The first refers to the historical persecution of the Jewish people who were forced to wander from land to land in their never-ending search for a haven from oppression. Another use of this term is the constant moving of Jewish neighborhoods from one location to another. One year may see a neighborhood inundated with Jewish residents. Kosher markets, day schools, synagogues and Jewish community centers will spiral up like blossoms in the spring. Suddenly, for clearly defined reasons or more subtle causes, the once flourishing neighborhood changes into a virtual ghost town over a short period of time.

One of the institutions which is greatly victimized by these shifts is the synagogue. A once heavily populated sanctuary, in all its luster and beauty, is quickly reduced to an edifice whose religious services are maintained by only a handful of diehards.

The new community which is quickly being inundated by the throngs of newcomers is generally faced with a problem. Regardless of specific affiliation, Jewish residents immediately seek a place to gather for worship. There are the daily services, holidays, Shabbat and the need to recite the *Kaddish* (memorial prayer). The forerunners quickly gather in a basement, store or home to commence the service schedule. Slowly, donations are solicited to begin the building effort. A new rabbi and cantor must be engaged and very expensive Torahs must be bought. Finally, pending the next exodus, the Jewish community is in place.

Taking all the above into consideration, I have conceived a plan which will save a huge amount of effort and expense. The book of Exodus

devotes a great deal of space and detail to the *Mishkan* (the Tabernacle), which was built shortly after the Children of Israel left Egypt and which accompanied them until the permanent houses of worship were built in Israel, culminating in the construction of the Holy Temple in Jerusalem. This *Mishkan* was brilliantly built to be a movable structure. The walls were made of curtains and all furnishings were constructed to be able to be lifted and carried by the Levites as they moved through the desert for forty years on their way to the Promised Land.

All of which led me to the idea that the ever-new Jewish communities should build their houses of worship designed after the biblical Sanctuary! All that would be required is the purchase of a parcel of land large enough to accommodate the transient edifice and provide for proper parking. Heating could be supplied by interior and external sources. The major expense would be a guard or two since the walls will be made of curtains.

Now that I have disclosed this novel idea, I await the appearance of the first portable synagogue!

Which Mountain is Holier?

Mounts Sinai and Moriah stand out as playing a prominent role in Jewish history. The former is the mountain upon which God gave the Ten Commandments. The latter is the place where Abraham was willing to offer his son for a sacrifice and where the two Holy Temples were built.

To me, it is of the greatest interest that the Torah itself states that as soon as the "all clear" was sounded after the Ten Commandments had been received, even the cattle could graze on the entire mountain. Apparently, there was no trace of sanctity left.

That is far from the situation of Mount Moriah. We are taught that its sanctity was relevant at the time of the two Holy Temples and remained for all time to come. When observant Jewish people go into the Temple area today, they must first immerse themselves in a *mikveh (*ritual bath) and carefully avoid stepping into the area which would be forbidden to them if the Holy Temple were in existence. Unlike Mount Sinai, its sanctity remained in full force.

This situation is somewhat surprising. After all, Mount Sinai became sacred through the direct presence of God Himself. Yet, the moment it was over, no trace of holiness remained. On Mount Moriah, however, the *kedusha (*sacredness) was of such intensity that it was to endure for all time.

I heard a possible solution to this seeming puzzle from Rabbi Immanuel Jakobovits, the late Chief Rabbi of the United Hebrew Congregations of the British Commonwealth (1921-1999). On one of his trips to the United States, he visited Providence, Rhode Island, and I had the opportunity of escorting him to Plymouth, home of the Plymouth Rock and the area from which America broke away from England to forge an independent nation. The rabbi was dressed quite formally with a black coat and an imposing "Homburg" hat. As we entered one of the stores, I could not resist the temptation to announce that, "This is the chief rabbi of the British Commonwealth. He is here to check how the colonies are getting on." Luckily, everyone took it in good cheer and we did not have to run for our lives.

It was at that time that the rabbi shared his opinion with me on the continued sanctity of Mount Moriah as compared to the short-lived one of Mount Sinai.

"When a father (Abraham) is willing to take his beloved son (Isaac), up to a mountain top to sacrifice him in response to a divine command, such ground becomes even more holy than the place where God appeared Himself." Thus, the sanctity attached to this mountain was never revoked.

Of course, it must be remembered that Jewish tradition teaches that it was on that very spot of the *Akedah* (the Binding of Isaac) that the Holy Temples were to be built.

It was a very satisfactory response and a memorable meeting with this eminent rabbi.

Jewish Concepts

If someone was determined to perform a mitzva and was prevented from doing so, Scripture credits him as if he had performed it. (Berachot 6a)

On Teleology

Teleology is a fascinating concept which has always been a fundamental belief in Judaism and continues to gain support with the advance of science. In short, it posits that everything in creation has a purpose.

The human body serves as a perfect example. There was a time when a number of organs were considered unnecessary and extraneous. To cite just one example, not too many years ago, tonsils were removed at the least irritation, usually when the child was at a young age. This practice was greatly curtailed when it was discovered that tonsils made a number of important contributions to the health and functioning of the human body.

The same holds true of the appendix. The very name of this organ suggests a superfluous item which somehow found its way into the human body. It, too, was removed at the slightest provocation. With the advent of greater medical knowledge, the appendix came to be removed only if its continued presence posed a danger to the health of the person.

There is a quaint and lovely Midrash which seeks to explain the groove in the middle of a baby's upper lip. It states that the child, prior to its birth, knew all the mysteries of the universe. In Jewish parlance, the child knew the entire Torah. Right before birth, an angel exerted pressure on this spot, which caused the baby to forget all this precious knowledge. How exciting and illuminating it would be if the angel overlooked just one infant!

The only exception that Jewish theology makes to teleology is the presence of the foreskin on the male organ. In fact, the Torah itself commands that this foreskin be removed on the eighth day of the life of a healthy baby boy.

At first glance, this would seem to fly right into the face of teleology. If every part of the body exists for a reason, what is this foreskin doing there in the first place? However, Judaism does not consider the presence of this membrane to be an accident in the total structure of the body. Strange as it may seem, we believe that it is there for the very purpose of being removed! Its presence is an indication of the fact that the world is still in an incomplete state and that a partnership between God and man will bring about the ultimate desired perfection. Not only is this symbolically accomplished through the removal of the physical foreskin, but it calls attention to the removal of the spiritual foreskin around the heart of each person. Through this removal, man in partnership with God, strives toward the ultimate perfection of creation.

It is my opinion that this concept of teleology is relevant to all creation. I refer specifically to the immense number of galaxies, stars and planets of which we are aware. It is probably only a fraction of what constitutes the universe at this relatively early stage of human knowledge.

If we believe that existence is not the result of mere chance, but part of a divine design, the question must occur to us as to what purpose these planets and galaxies serve. Did they just haphazardly fall into their places or is their presence part of a master plan, and perhaps more importantly, do they perform a service or need? Did they come into existence for a purpose in the past, in the present, or will they perform a function in the future?

It is my firm belief that just as the present world has shrunk due to the ever-increasing speed of aerial travel, the time between earth and the innumerable planets will constantly decrease. Man has already walked upon the moon and the continuation of these voyages is only a matter of time.

Of course, it will demand a huge amount of scientific ingenuity to create conditions to sustain life on other planets, but history has shown that no obstacles ultimately stand in the way of man's continuous growth of knowledge.

The immediate benefit of such progress will be an end to any problems of over -population. There will be more than enough space for all and the varying climates and other conditions will probably give people a choice of where they want to spend their lives.

But there is room for much deeper consideration about which we can only speculate. If we accept the concept of teleology, that everything that has been created has its purpose, perhaps some existence is temporary, while other existence is eternal. The sheer mass of such existence, past, present and future, totally staggers the human imagination and cannot begin to be quantified within our present frames of reference. To somewhat allay our possible frustration, we need only consider the power of the computer. Its capability of collating and harnessing huge amounts of miniscule data in split seconds is but a tiny indication of infinite possibilities. Ancient man would never have believed our present accomplishments, as we would not believe what the future is going to unfold.

I would find it difficult to believe that the staggering amount of existence, of which we are becoming more and more aware, is the result of a haphazard accident or series of such. It seems far more reasonable to believe that God created the universe and saw that it was good. Every blade of grass came into being for a purpose, as did you and I. It seems that we have only touched the surface. The rest and best is yet to come.

Who Turned on the Lights?

There is a Jewish regulation, known in Hebrew as *marit ayin* (as it appears to the eye), which, in general terms, refers to the creation of a wrong impression. For example, a Jewish man should not stand in front of a theatre on Shabbat because he may create the impression that he had attended the performance. This precaution is prevalent in many halachic areas.

An interesting such problem arose with the development of what is today known as the "Shabbat clock." This instrument is simply an automatic timer. The control panel can be adjusted to turn on lights or extinguish them at pre-adjusted times. If programmed before Shabbat, the lights will go on and off as desired.

Before the discovery of electricity, candles were the medium by which light pervaded the Jewish home. Although these candles were romanticized to bring peace and tranquility into the home, its other very pragmatic use was to provide the necessary light for the meal before people retired.

As can well be imagined, electric lighting was a great bonus. But it arrived with a problem. Once the light was turned on and Shabbat had arrived, it could no longer be turned off. How could one fall asleep in the glaring light? What about the cost of excessive use of electricity? Nevertheless, the Halacha was clear. The rabbis had decided that the properties of electricity sufficiently resembled those of fire to warrant prohibiting their being generated or extinguished on the Sabbath. Could anything be done?

It seemed that with the advent of the "Shabbat clock," all problems would be solved. One major problem emerged, however, which placed the entire project into jeopardy - *marit ayin*. People strolling on the streets would see lights going on and off in Jewish homes. The electric timers were still generally unknown, and, therefore, there was a distinct possibility that people might assume that the Sabbath was being violated by people who were known to be Sabbath observing Jews!

The way this dilemma became resolved seems to be reasonably clear. Those who first made use of this clock simply disregarded any suspicions that might be directed at them. They continued to do so as others joined them until it eventually became a universally accepted practice. The Shabbat clock became a recognized device and there was no more possible suspicion.

It seems that there must always be some pioneers who are undisturbed by what people may think until such a time that it becomes clear to all.

Perhaps it would be appropriate to inject a final thought into this matter. I knew a wonderful man by the name of Cantor Abraham Schonfeld, who was warm and friendly to all. He did not have much use for this entire concept of *marit ayin*. He felt that no Jewish laws should be developed because of people's negative suspicions of others. Should we not judge all people according to merit?

Should we not, indeed?

Love can be a Halachic Imperative

When we refer to love, we conjure up a state of warm feelings toward another person, object or idea. However, there is an area where the concept of love falls into a strict halachic category. I refer to a *Kohen* (Priest) who is about to extend his benediction upon the people. He must preface this sacred act with the following blessing:

> "Blessed are You … who sanctified us with His commandments and commanded us to bless His people with *love*."

Note that the text concludes with the condition that the blessing the *Kohen* is about to extend to the congregation must be accompanied by love. Jewish law clearly defines this requirement by teaching that if the *Kohen* feels hatred to even a single person among those gathered, he must disqualify himself.

This contains a powerful lesson. The absence of love toward a group or individual can cause very practical and unwanted ramifications. Instead of excusing himself from carrying out this important *mitzva*, it would be so much better if the *Kohen* were to make an effort to settle his differences with the person whom he dislikes and resume the blessing which he is to offer to benefit all the people.

In the same manner, each and every one of us would be well advised to do the same. We are taught that the second Holy Temple was destroyed because of senseless hatred. Each act of seeking to undo such injurious emotions will add another brick in the third and final Temple.

No Daily Blessing

One of the great opportunities I look forward to when I am in Israel is the daily blessing of the *Kohanim* (men who are descendants of Aaron the Priest) to the congregation. On Shabbat and festivals, this blessing is also extended during the *Mussaf* (Additional) service. After their hands are ritually washed by the Levites (a first-born in the absence of a Levi), the *Kohanim* are summoned and, as the people bow their heads, they chant the traditional blessing as they have been commanded by the Torah. Many fathers in the congregation follow the beautiful custom of covering their children's heads with their *tallit* during this ceremony.

The entire ritual is based upon the following commandment in the Torah:

> And God spoke to Moses, saying, "Speak to Aaron and his sons, saying, 'So shall you bless the Children of Israel. May God bless you and safeguard you. May God cause His countenance to shine upon you and be gracious unto you. May God lift His countenance upon you and grant you peace.'" (Numbers 6:23)

Since the Torah is clear that this blessing is to be delivered by the *Kohanim* without qualification, it seems difficult to understand why it is correctly chanted on a daily basis in Israel, but only on a very limited basis in all countries outside of Israel. It should be noted that the Sephardic custom is to have the *Kohanim* bless the people everywhere, not just in Israel.

The traditional response is that there is a greater degree of *simcha* (joy) in Israel, especially because of the proximity to the Holy Temple area and that is why this blessing is more valid in the Holy Land than in countries removed from this region.

Far be it from me to question decisions made by the great Sages of Israel and I would never consider having these benedictions rendered in my synagogue except on permitted days. I have rationalized the absence of this blessing to perhaps demonstrate the difference between Israel and the *Galut* (Diaspora). Nevertheless, it has always seemed problematic to me that so many are being deprived of a blessing which was directly commanded by the Torah to the *Kohanim,* without any exclusions. I hope that one day, this custom will be changed.

The Rich Need Blessing

The blessings conveyed by the *Kohanim* (descendants of Aaron) are divided into three sections. The first of these states, "May the Lord bless you and watch over you" (Numbers 6:23). Some commentaries teach that this part of the tri-sectional blessing is directed toward those who are wealthy. One may well wonder why this group requires a special blessing. After all, they have attained so much monetary gain that one would think that their riches are their blessing. What else do they require?

The traditional response is that the affluent are in danger of becoming arrogant, slothful and insensitive to others. They might treat wealth as a shield which exempts them from having to exercise the proper manners and respect due to their fellow human beings. They are also in danger of becoming jealous of rich contemporaries, thereby always seeking to increase their wealth over others. One is often shocked to hear of the most wealthy being involved in illegal activities in an effort to expand their riches.

All of which brings to mind the deep and meaningful advice in *Pirkei Avot*, "Who is wealthy? He who is happy (satisfied) with his lot" (Ethics of the Fathers 4:1).

Thus we see the need for a special blessing by the *Kohanim* to protect them from these negative tendencies so that they may utilize their riches for good purposes in a tranquil spirit.

It seems to me that there is another dimension to the extra blessing which the wealthy require. The riches which they enjoy are far from a free ride. Responsibilities evolve upon them which are not relevant to those of lesser means. Of course, their major responsibilities lie in acts of *tzedaka,* generally translated as charity, but which actually means righteousness. They have a clear obligation to help the poor in every possible way. But that responsibility falls upon all of us even if the amounts that poorer people are able to contribute are far less than that of the wealthy.

Yet another possible area of assistance is to family members. This is not an actual requirement, but rather an act of goodwill and benevolence by those relatives who are materially able to share and extend this benefit.

This proffering of a friendly hand is best expressed by the verse:

"Behold, how good and pleasant it is for brothers (siblings) to dwell together" (Psalm 123:1).

I find this verse to have far greater implications than an idyllic description of society. I see in it some very real and practical applications. If interpreted literally, it could mean that all members of a family should ideally live on the same standard. In others words, if one relative attains riches and is able to help other family members, then it is *tov* (good) and *na'im* (proper) for him to do so. The wording of the verse is very precise. The rich person is obligated to give *tzedaka* to family members only if they are in need. However, even if *tzedaka* is not required, helping them raise their standard of living is considered "good" and "proper."

The word *gam* (also) in the verse is also significant. To me, it implies that if one family member has been blessed with riches, then his brothers should *also* be helped to live on an equal level.

Of course, this ethical choice would only apply if the rich relative is not adversely affected by this aid and if the recipient accepts the help as a gift given happily to enable all the family members to live in reasonable equality.

I have seen an example of a man who had amassed a great deal of wealth. His sister managed to live a modest middle class lifestyle with her husband and children. A widowed mother was involved. The man bought them a beachside summer home and helped his sister develop a real estate business by underwriting the purchase of a number of buildings. Halachically, the brother had absolutely no obligation to expend any of his money in this fashion. But it was *tov* (good) and *na'im* (proper) for him to do so. Through his thoughtfulness and generosity, the "brothers dwelled together," on the same level. It should also be added that the rich sibling was not at all financially strained by these contributions; his wealth far exceeded these expenditures.

There is a very interesting and subtle allusion to this matter in the Torah itself. I refer to the verse which recounts the blessing of Moses to the following two tribes:

"Rejoice, Zevulun, on your journeys and Issachar, in your tents" (Deuteronomy 33:18).

This blessing has traditionally been interpreted as one brother, Issachar, who excelled as a merchant, funding his scholarly brother, Zevulun, who dedicated his life to the study of Torah. While the basis of this example speaks in favor of supporting the study of Torah, it nevertheless also demonstrates how brothers can utilize the opportunity to help not only other siblings, but members of the family as a whole.

One other exception to this rule is the care of parents. This is included in the fifth of the ten commandments and is not optional, but incumbent upon children.

Thus, we see that the blessing of the *Kohanim* referring to the wealthy has many ramifications. Anyone who has been blessed with an abundance of wealth has the opportunity to increase tranquility and goodwill in the family through this prosperity. It is truly sad to see friction caused by financial conflicts in all too many families. If a rich relative uses his resources to bring prosperity to his family, the blessings directed toward him will have come to total fruition.

The Power of a Blessing or Curse

There is evidence in our tradition that a blessing or curse, even if pronounced unintentionally, could result in its unintended effect. For example, in the book of *Bereshit* (Genesis), we read how Isaac unwittingly blessed his son Jacob, instead of his older son Esau, and could not retract the blessing.

An example of an unintended curse resulting in the premature death of Rachel, the wife of Jacob, occurred when Laban was searching for the *teraphim* which Rachel had secretly taken from him. Jacob said to him in anger, "With whomever you find these items, he shall not live" (Genesis 31:32). Jacob had no idea that his curse was unintentionally directed at his beloved wife. Rashi states that it was because of this curse that Rachel died prematurely in Bethlehem.

The Talmud is also very clear on this subject.

"Let not the blessing of (even) a simple person be insignificant in your eyes" (Tractate *Megilla* 15a).

Which brings me to a dilemma I faced when reciting *Birkat Hamazon* (Grace After the Meal) in a crowded restaurant in Jerusalem's Central Bus Station. The tables were filled with diners totally unknown to me. I felt sure that most, if not all, of those seated around me, were good people whom I wished to include in the prayer which states, "May the compassionate One bless all those who are dining here."

Now, it may be argued that only those sitting at my table are included in my blessing, but even at one large table, there may be people who are unknown to me. On a broader scale, why can't my blessing be extended to all those in a huge restaurant? The answer is simply because evil people or even terrorists could benefit from this blessing, though my prayer was certainly not intended to include them.

Does this mean that I have to restrain myself from a deep desire to bestow a blessing on all the people around me?

I discussed this matter at length with my grandson, Daniel Eisenstock, and we came to what I consider a very satisfactory solution.

Our Rabbis teach that one must be precise in one's prayers. Therefore, I suggest that a proper blessing would state, "*ve'et kol ha'anashim ha'kesherim hamesubim kahn*," ("and all the *upright* people who are dining here").

This is far from being pedantic. The above examples from the Torah demonstrate that a blessing or curse, even if unintentional, could well become a reality. By adding this disclaimer, I can extend my sincere blessings to all the people I love in the hope that they will be consummated.

But I Didn't Do It!

There is an apparent difficulty in the *vidui* (confession) of the Yom Kippur (Day of Atonement) service. In fact, this problem is evident in all our confessional prayers. They are in the plural. The general text is, "We have sinned, we have transgressed." On Yom Kippur, the list is even more specific. We read, for example, "For the sin which we have sinned before You through evil talk," etc.

We are taught to be very careful in our admission of sin, to be truthful and forthright. It is only through admission of the enactment of a wrongdoing that we can express regret for the act and not repeat it. However, the litany of transgressions to which we openly admit seems to fly in the face of this teaching.

Let us take the above confession as an example. There are those good people who studiously avoid speaking ill of others. They immediately terminate such talk and, if unsuccessful, leave the company of the gossipers. They refuse to even listen. Now would it be a sincere admission of guilt by such a person to ask forgiveness for the sin of "evil talk"?

While the question seems to be very telling, the response is a virtual revelation. When pleading guilty to the sins perpetrated by many, we affirm that, to a degree, *we are all responsible for each other*. Thus, for example, if we hear a person making wrongful allegations about another, we are somewhat responsible. Perhaps we could say the right thing at the right time to put a stop to it. In other words, we should not only be accountable for our own personal actions, but we should try to be involved in those of others as well.

This point may be proven by the fact that personal confession must be done discreetly. Judaism does not permit confession to any other human being. It must be a direct declaration to God. How, then, can all these confessions be stated publicly? The answer is because they reflect our communal responsibility. When someone sins, we are all somewhat guilty because of our obligation to each other. Personal sins must be declared quietly and privately.

Communal responsibility is a wonderful and essential concept which binds us to each other. In the final analysis, we are one people under one God.

A Case for Teshuva

One of the key rules in the area of *kashrut* (dietary laws) is the principal of *bitul* (nullification). While each case must be examined individually, there is a rule that if a forbidden food inadvertently falls into a permitted mixture, it may lose its identity if there are sixty parts of that which is permitted against the offending particle. Once such a *bitul* has taken place, the entire mixture is again permitted for consumption.

While this is a well-known fact, there is a very interesting and revealing side issue to this matter. Let us assume, at least theoretically, that another non-kosher particle falls into this new mixture. We would again need a composition of sixty against one to render it permissible. But now, the first non-kosher particle, more than just having lost its identity *becomes a force in its own right to render the mixture kosher*!

I believe that one can learn a great lesson from the above physical reaction. If a person becomes a sincere *baal teshuva* (repentant), he does not merely bring himself into a new dimension of spirituality, but he is a changed person who can now exert a positive influence for the betterment of all.

Lead us into Temptation

N o, I did not inadvertently leave out the word "not" from the title. The popularity of the phrase, "Lead us not into temptation" is nothing less than universal. Yet, it does not conform to traditional Jewish belief. To us, temptation is a challenge which must always be present and overcome. Without it, man is not the human being he was created to be. His actions would be reflexive, not the result of free choice, and would have little meaning.

This is not only true of man's actions, but of countless practical examples. A prime instance is that of *chametz,* the leavening which must be discarded before Passover. Now it could be asked why we must go to all the trouble of producing *matza,* the unleavened bread which is eaten on Passover, with just those five grains which can easily become leavened. Why not use other grains for *matza* and avoid all the bother and potential problems?

But that is just the point. In order to be the kind of "bread" which may be used for Passover, there has to be the *possibility* for it to become *chametz* in a very short time and it is this danger which has to be overcome.

Consider all of man's activities. His basic animalistic instinct is to grab food and gulp it down. Yet this base disposition is overcome by the ritual washing of the hands, the Grace After Meal and other commandments, thereby making the institution of eating a pleasant, meaningful and even spiritual act.

The same holds true of procreation. The spontaneous instinct would be to couple in an animalistic manner and procreate instinctively. Yet, the Torah and our traditions have elevated this physical act into a sublime and transcendent one upon which our very families and communal lives are based.

Earning a living is an area replete with halachic considerations. Again, animalistic temptation and reflex would have us grab anything within our reach or seek to gain riches dishonestly. It is by overcoming these enticements that we achieve a life of honest income and sharing with our fellow human beings.

The inducement to do that which tempts us is a necessary and constant companion in every phase of our lives. Our ongoing effort to always face and overcome this *Yetzer Hara (*Evil Inclination*)* is what defines us as human beings in general and observant Jews in particular.

A simple example of the above is the heart-warming story of an elderly man who arose very early each morning during the freezing days of winter to get to the synagogue in time for the *Shacharit (*morning) service. He was questioned about this determination. Due to his advanced age, he was advised to occasionally remain in bed until the winter passed and the weather became milder.

"I'm afraid I will have to continue to get up as early as usual," he responded. "You see, my Evil Inclination is as old as I am. He has been with me since my birth. Now, I can't begin to tell you how persistent he is even in his advanced age. He never lets up in his attempts to have me waver from my responsibilities. That being the case, I am going to be just as determined and will continue to rise up early in the morning!"

Overcoming temptation is our constant challenge. Succeeding is our greatest satisfaction.

Bagel Seeds

One of the most widely known blessings is that of "*Hamotzi lechem min ha'aretz*," which is recited prior to eating bread. Even the most untutored person in Jewish prayers will happily accept the invitation to lead the guests in reciting this blessing prior to a banquet at a wedding or bar mitzva.

It seems that very few have apparently given thought to these familiar words. Essentially, we are thanking God for bringing forth bread out of the ground, but has anyone actually ever seen *bread* breaking through the earth as do vegetables? Is it possible to purchase bagel, rye or challah seeds? In short, is this blessing reflecting reality?

A possible answer to this question is that the blessing, as presently constructed, is both a hope and a prophecy. There is a tradition that prior to Adam and Eve's sin of eating from the Tree of Knowledge, bread actually did grow as a finished product. Adam and Eve did not have to go through the tedious process of grinding the wheat, mixing it with water and yeast and finally baking the dough. Everything was ready for them to enjoy.

Once they committed the sin of eating from the Tree of Knowledge, it was decreed that they must now work for their sustenance. Instead of the finished product of bread continuing to grow from the ground, they now had to engage in the labors required to produce this staple of life.

Nevertheless, we continue to recite the blessing reminiscent of its original meaning, when the finished bread actually appeared as a finished product. And we do this for good reason. It is based on our hope that mankind will one day return to the Garden of Eden. After all, the Garden of Eden was not destroyed. It remained intact with the *Cherubim* posted to guard its entrance. Had the intent been for man never to return, it would surely have been obliterated. That being the case, we should always strive to return to the Garden of Eden and obtain all its benefits, not the least of which will be to enjoy the bread which will again grow right out of the ground.

Glatt Versus Super-Glatt

T he term "Glatt," ("smooth") refers to the lungs of a kosher animal, properly slaughtered and being devoid of any defects, such as adhesions. If such a situation occurred some decades ago, a competent rabbinical authority was consulted to determine if the lesions caused the animal to be prohibited or permitted. According to Rabbi Moshe Isserlis (the *Rema*), there are adhesions which will not render the animal *treiff* (non-kosher). This was the historical manner in which meat was prepared for Jewish communities throughout the centuries.

Over the past few decades, a number of fundamental changes occurred. As soon as any lesions or possible defects were discovered on the lung of an animal, many authorities automatically declared it as not "Glatt," as a result of which it was not acceptable. The fallout of this new approach was that many slaughtered animals which would clearly have been declared kosher by competent experts, were now looked upon with disdain by those who subscribed to the new category of "Glatt."

Another interesting development was that the term "Glatt" came to be applied to non-meat products, such as chicken, fish and, in extreme situations – even water! Entire establishments, such as restaurants now advertise themselves as being "Glatt Kosher."

All the above is not to imply that there is only one universal "Glatt" product. Far from it. Many of the major *kashrut* agencies compete with each other in promoting their own "Glatt Kosher" products.

One of the most common disclaimers heard today when a hotel, restaurant or other eating establishment comes to the forefront in a discussion is, "I don't eat there;" "That place does not seem right;" "I noticed that a lot of people eat there without a *kippa* (head cover)."

At times, it seems as if the whole matter seems to be one of personal validation and justification, followed by an attempt to outdo all others.

Perhaps a note of humor can be injected into this not so humorous development.

A very devout man lived to a ripe old age after which he passed on. Because of the saintly life he led, a large welcome was prepared for him in *Olam Haba* (the World to Come). A sumptuous banquet was arranged composed of the finest meats, poultry and delectable dishes of every description.

Looking at all the foods, the honoree asked his neighbor, "Tell me, who is the *Mashgiach* (religious food supervisor) here?"

"What a question!" came the emphatic response. "This is Heaven. None other than the Holy One, blessed be He is the *Mashgiach* here!"

A distrustful frown formed on the man's face. "Then I think I'll just have a glass of tea."

We would do well to keep in mind the famous teaching of the prophet Micah, "And what does God require of you? To act justly and to love mercy and to walk humbly with your God" (Micah 6:8).

Tallit Over the Head

The *tallit*, worn by men during the morning prayers, is generally referred to as a prayer shawl. It is a good translation because the word "shawl" correlates to the Hebrew word "to wrap." This reflects the proper way to don the *tallit*. It is swung over one's head, after which it is wrapped around the shoulders, there to remain until the conclusion of the prayers.

The size of the *tallit* has come a long way. I remember those very thin and skimpy *tallesim* that would fill the racks for visitors to take upon entry in the lobby. There were also the more traditional woolen ones which covered the majority of one's back. The men who frequented the synagogues on a limited basis invariably chose the skimpy ones, while the heavier ones found their places on the shoulders of the regular worshippers. This custom has changed a great deal. Apparently, most men have become comfortable with the larger versions and the skimpier ones have all but disappeared.

However, a new phenomenon developed which has come to be universally accepted in Orthodox synagogues today. I refer to a reasonably large percentage of men who place the *tallit* over their heads during various parts of the service. As I look back over the years, especially to the time when I was a young boy through my teens, this was a custom relegated to extremely few individuals. In fact, even most rabbis and cantors, to the best of my recollection, refrained from covering their heads in this manner. In most congregations, there were usually one or two men, well advanced in age and renowned for their wisdom and piety, who sat in the front section of the sanctuary and quietly and reverentially offered their prayers. The congregants treated them with great respect. These were the only ones who would cover their heads with the *tallit*.

I have no idea what precipitated the change, but within a short period of time, it was hard to recognize fellow congregants because their faces were all but concealed. It seems to have become the modern style. This new fashion is especially widespread among the many *baalei teshuva* (repentants).

It was difficult for me to follow this trend. I admit that I very occasionally gave it a try, but felt very self-conscious and inadequate. Quite frankly, I did not feel sufficiently "holy." However, I did make one concession. Being an officiating rabbi, I stood right under the *Kohanim* (priestly class) when they blessed the congregation. It is forbidden to look at them during those sacred moments. I decided to cover my head with the *tallit* during this ceremony. After a while, I became comfortable with this arrangement and now do it wherever I happen to be.

It is important that I am not misunderstood in this matter. In no way am I critical of anyone, even a youngster, who chooses to cover his head with his *tallit*. If this aids him in finding greater spirituality during prayer, he certainly should do it. I merely am commenting on a major change which took place in a comparatively short period and thought it would be interesting to point out.

What is Techelet?

The commandment to wear *tzitzit* (knotted ritual fringes), appears twice in the Torah.

> And God said to Moses: "Speak to the Children of Israel and say to them that they shall make for themselves *tzitzit* (fringes) on the corners of their garments, throughout their generations. And they shall place upon the *tzitzit* of each corner a thread of **techelet**. And they shall be *tzitzit* for you, that you may see and remember all the commandments of God and remember them." (Numbers 15:38, 39)

> You shall make for yourselves twisted threads on the four corners of your garment with which you cover yourself. (Deuteronomy 22:12)

The Torah clearly states the reason for these fringes. They are meant to accustom the viewer to remember the commandments imposed by the Torah. In ancient times, these fringes were attached to the four corners of the clothing which were worn by men. When the styles changed and suits no longer had these four corners, the *tallit* (prayer shawl) was substituted during prayer and the *tallit katan* (four-cornered undergarment) was equipped with *tzitzit*.

Four long threads are inserted into a hole on each corner of the garment. For many centuries, three were white and one was the color of a specific shade of blue called *techelet*. These threads were doubled over, leaving eight strings on each of the four corners. They were then knotted according to a number of traditions.

It was important that the hue of blue mandated by the Torah be exactly as it was commanded. The accepted source of this color is a mollusk (marine creature) identified in the Talmud (*Menachot* 44a*)* as the *chilazon*. Its secretion was the source for the required shade known as *techelet*.

Sometime after the destruction of the second Holy Temple, the identity of the *chilazon* was lost. Since that time, for almost two thousand years, all the tassels of the *tzitzit* were only white. Since the exact hue mandated by the Torah was no longer known, it was deemed best to leave the threads in their natural state of white.

This situation changed somewhat in 1887 with the Radziner Rav (Rabbi Gershom Henoch Leiner), who was very knowledgeable in science and worked tirelessly for the restoration of the *techelet*. After much study on sea creatures, he concluded that the required bluish hue stemmed from a squid known as the cuttlefish. He defended his discovery with a number of learned works. All his disciples adopted his version of *techelet,* as did a number of eminent rabbis and many Breslov *Chasidim* (disciples). Many leading contemporary rabbis, however, opposed his findings.

There was little change in this status quo until 1985 when Otto Eisner, a chemist at the Shenker College of Fibers in Israel proved that a sky-blue could be produced from the secretion of the Murex snail. This assertion was supported by a chemical analysis made on a fabric recovered from Masada in the 1960's.

The entire matter took a firm stand in 1988 when Rabbi Eliyahu Tauger dyed *techelet* from the Murex dye. The *Ptil Techelet* organization was founded to produce and educate in all matters of this *mitzva*.

It must be noted that there are very respectable opinions that oppose simply picking up an ancient practice such as *techelet* after centuries of disuse. Nevertheless, there are now large communities in Israel and elsewhere where the *techelet* threads have become a prominent part of the *tallit*. The methods of their being knotted together follows varying traditions.

I have no doubt that when the modern renewal of this *mitzva* will become more accepted, revelations will support its acceptance and we will be that much closer to our ultimate Redemption.

Out of Line

Joining a prestigious country club was a goal to which many Jews aspired on their climb up the social ladder. This was not always an easy task since many of the more exclusive clubs had policies which effectively barred Jewish applicants. I do not know how that matter stands today, but my story reflects the reverse.

A very friendly gentile lived in an upscale Jewish neighborhood and wanted to join a country club whose membership was mainly Jewish. His goal was to befriend many of his neighbors who were members of the club. Not to stand out, he decided to pass himself off as being Jewish.

"What do you think would be a good occupation for me to make interesting conversation?" he asked a friend. "I'm thinking of something in the Jewish field."

"I have an idea," came the response. "Tell them you manufacture *tallesim* (prayer shawls)."

The idea seemed a good one and after a few weeks, our friend found himself sitting at a table, having dinner with his new circle of friends.

"So what do you do for a living?" came the inevitable question.

Bob was prepared. "I manufacture *tallesim,*" he glibly replied.

"I'm so glad to hear that," responded one of the diners. "I've always wondered about something. Those black lines that run along the length of the *tallit* are as straight as a ruler. How do you manage that?"

Somewhat flustered, our friend replied, "I wouldn't know. I only make the sleeves."

Is the Kippa Holy?

As I was walking along one of the streets of Efrat in Israel on a breezy day, I noticed that a strong burst of wind blew the *kippa* (yarmulke) off the head of a young boy. He quickly ran to catch it and, before replacing it back on his head, gave it a perfunctory kiss. This was not the first time I have seen this form of respect accorded to this type of head covering and it gave me a moment of thought.

The covering of the head of Jewish males is universally accepted by traditional Jewish men throughout the world. Since the State of Israel came into being, a wide variety of *kippot* have appeared of every description. There are the traditional black ones, the knitted type and unique other patterns of every form and description. Even those men who do not regularly wear a *kippa* will be sure to do so when entering a Jewish sanctuary.

All of which could well lead one to wonder what the actual standing of this little head covering is in terms of sanctity and Halacha (Jewish law).

On the humorous level, the question is asked, "How do you know that wearing a *kippa* is mandated by the Torah?"

"That is quite simple," goes the reply. "The Torah informs us that Moses was walking. Now can you imagine that Moses would have walked without a *kippa*?"

Despite its universal acceptance, the fact remains that the *kippa* does not possess any intrinsic sanctity. Unlike the *tallit* (prayer shawl) and *tefillin* (phylacteries), no blessings are recited when donning the *kippa* and nothing need be done to treat it as a sacred object.

Certainly the boy did nothing wrong by kissing his head covering after scooping it off the ground. He was simply reflecting the immense acceptance of this custom among the Jewish people. While not attributing any sanctity to the *kippa*, Jewish law takes this head covering quite seriously and teaches that one must cover his head while walking, eating and praying. It has become the Jewish way of showing respect and being aware of the ever-present divine sanctity.

Judaism teaches that a *minhag* (custom) can actually become stronger than a law. That is exactly what happened in the evolution of the *kippa*. From remote beginnings, the concept grew among the people, although the object itself did not assume any form of holiness. There are no rules as to the shape or material of the head covering. However, the covered head is reflective of the Jewish form of respect to God and to all that is sacred.

Spiritual Blood Pressure

The story is told of an observant Jew who was admitted to a hospital. In the morning, he donned his *tefillin* (phylacteries). As he turned the straps around his arm, the other patient in the room stared at him and said to the nurse, "I always knew Jews were smart, but to take your own blood pressure like that."

I find that there is a little more to this joke than meets the eye. Because the truth of the matter is that when the *tefillin* are wrapped around the arm and placed upon the forehead, there definitely is a measure being taken of the *spiritual* pressure of the individual.

A Tzadik and a Chasid

A person on a high spiritual level is generally referred to as a *Tzadik*. However, there is another description which is often used with the same intent - and that is the appellation of *Chasid*. While both terms are intended as being complimentary, they are really not identical and it is interesting to ascertain their true meaning by pointing out the difference.

Technically, a *Tzadik* does nothing above or beyond what is required of him. The word derives from *tzedek,* which means righteousness. Of course, someone who is able to accomplish all or a great part of what the Jewish rules require of him, is on an extremely high spiritual rung. However, it must be remembered that he is not doing anything beyond what he is called upon to achieve, lofty as the goal may be.

The other term, *Chasid,* is quite different. It should not be confused with the Chasidic sects that sprung up with the advent of the founder of Chasidism, the *Baal Shem Tov* (Rabbi Yisrael ben Eliezer – 1698-1760). Many Chasidic sects were founded and proliferated after him. Adherents of all these movements came to be known as *Chasidim* and also assumed the name of each specific group to which they adhered.

The *Chasid* referred to here need not belong to any specific group. The title does not refer to his affiliation, but rather to his character. He is obviously a very fine and observant person. But how does he differ from the *Tzadik?*

The Hebrew word, *chesed*, actually implies "excess." This could refer to positive or negative attributes. It may be somewhat surprising that this word is found in the Torah with a very negative connotation.

117

> A man who takes his sister, the daughter of his father or mother, and sees her nakedness ... it is a chesed and he shall be cut off from his people. (Leviticus 20:17)

It would seem surprising, almost shocking, that the Torah would refer to such an abominable act of incest as one of *chesed*. In this case, however, the meaning is that one has completely gone over the boundary and committed an act of totally excessive immorality.

The same definition applies to acts of goodness. The *Chasid*, in his desire to commit acts of benefit and charity, goes further than *tzedek* - beyond the call of Jewish law - and devotes himself to acts above and beyond any requirements. This is the definition of a *Chasid*.

It is certainly a fine line that differentiates between these two pious and dedicated people, but it is quite useful to understand what gives each one his unique characteristics. Of course, it is not up to us to judge anyone. We believe that there is only one true Judge. Nevertheless, even when we take spiritual stock of ourselves, it is interesting to note that if we are within the boundaries of what our duties are, we are engaging in *tzedek*. If we manage to go above and beyond the line of duty in an effort to serve God on a higher level or make an extra effort to help our fellow human beings, we are practicing *chesed*.

Fleecing the Congregation

While staying in Jerusalem for a number of weeks, I went to the synagogue which was only a few minutes from my apartment. It did not take me long to notice that except for Shabbat, morning prayers were virtually inundated by "collectors" from the beginning to the end of the prayers. The gleaners of this charity came in all forms. Most were bearded with the cloak of *Chasidim* who approached the worshippers with an extended hand. Some held up a document stating that they were collecting for a specific cause or were in need of personal support. Others were dressed in contemporary clothing holding a walking stick or simply extending their hands.

The congregants were completely accustomed to these collectors. In fact, many had coins prepared which, amid their prayers, they distributed on a first-come, first-served basis.

I have memories of this situation being rampant at the Kotel (the Western Wall) in Jerusalem quite some years ago. The entire plaza was teeming with hordes of beggars who were strident and, at times, simply refused a donation because it was not sufficiently large. Somehow, the authorities managed to put a stop to this and now one is only surreptitiously greeted by an open hand. This simply moved the begging from the plaza in front of the Wall to the surrounding areas.

I have studiously avoided making any judgments on these matters since I do not have all the required information. There is little doubt in my mind that there is a significant percentage of charlatans among them, but there are also those who are sincere and needy in their quest for alms. I do not know why government and other agencies cannot or do not provide for them. I distribute coins in the synagogue and do not question those who are seeking them. But I ask myself why this practice is prevalent mainly in religious circles and, at least transparently, the collectors are religious. I have never seen this drill at, for example, a concert or secular lecture.

There is no question that the institution of *tzedaka* (charity) ranks very high among Jewish values. In fact, the Rabbis describe it as one of the main pillars upon which the world rests. The correct translation of the word is actually "righteousness," not "charity." Sharing one's wealth with the poor is not considered a matter of choice; it is a spiritual imperative.

There is, however, a responsibility on the part of those who are seeking help from the more fortunate. Such help may only be requested under the proper conditions and in a respectful manner. To support this assertion, I refer to Maimonides, who was certainly a great proponent of giving *tzedaka*. In fact, he legislated the basis of how much a person should contribute and under what conditions. Thus, it should be very instructive to read what he had to say about the above situations.

> One who makes up his mind to involve himself with Torah and not to work and to support himself from *tzedaka*, has profaned God's name and brought Torah into contempt, extinguishing the light of religion, brought evil upon himself, and has taken away his life from the World to Come. (*Hilchot Talmud Torah* 3:10)

I repeat that I do not have the solution to the problem. I appreciate the words of Maimonides of how demeaning this is to the people, the Torah and all connected with it. Perhaps the day will come when it will be brought to a stop. In the meantime, let me close this less than happy subject with a humorous anecdote.

A couple were extremely rich and living in luxury. However, the financial market suddenly turned and they were left in dire poverty. So bad was their situation that they were forced to collect alms door-to-door. After quite some time, they were in the middle of a street where they were collecting. An excited man came running after them shouting that the market had turned back in their favor and they were wealthy once again. The wife looked at her husband and said, "Let's just finish this block."

That Controversial Sheitel

Modesty is one of the cornerstones of Judaism and it is reflected in both physical appearance and psychological restraint. Our books of proper behavior are replete with advice on the bearing of an unassuming and humble attitude toward others.

Being clothed in an appropriate manner is included in the scope of this requirement. One of the areas specifically focused upon is that of women's hair, especially after marriage. The Talmudic sages describe a woman's hair as being a source for *erva* (cause for eliciting inappropriate thoughts and feelings).

While a woman's hair as being a basis of *erva* is not mentioned explicitly in the Torah, a hint may be found in the section on the *Sotah,* a married woman suspected by her husband of adultery. To determine her guilt or innocence, she must undergo a ceremony. The following verse, describing part of this ceremony, sheds light on this matter.

"The *Kohen* shall have the woman stand before God and uncover the woman's head" (Numbers 5:18).

Rashi points out the fact, in the name of the Sages, that the need for the uncovering of the woman's hair demonstrates that it is improper for a married woman to be publicly seen bareheaded.

There is another verse in the Torah which might indicate that even a woman's face must be covered. I refer to the first meeting of Isaac with his wife-to-be, Rebecca.

> And Rebecca raised her eyes and saw Isaac. And she said to
> the servant, "Who is that man in the field walking toward

us?" And the servant said, "He is my master." She then took the scarf and covered herself. (Genesis 24:64, 65)

The Hebrew word *"tza'if"* means scarf and is a clear indication that Rebecca covered part of her face. Yet, as I perused the commentaries, I did not find any support for the fact that women would not let themselves be seen in public unless their faces were covered. At most, they suggested that Rebecca did this in deference to her future husband. My only intention in bringing this matter up is to illustrate that there may be varying sources of *erva* at different times and in varying societies.

There are many methods for an observant woman to conceal her hair in public. Perhaps, from a historical point of view, the *sheitel* may have been paramount in achieving this goal in modern times. I remember that this was my mother's custom throughout her married life.

There are many Jewish movements, such as Lubavitch, which encourage women to utilize the *sheitel* exclusively.

This is hardly the practice in the Israeli circles where my daughters currently live. In their very large community, very few women wear *sheitel*s. Rather, they observe the tradition with the use of colorful kerchiefs, berets and hats.

Of course, it is not necessarily the method, but the achievement of the goal which is most important. However, I would like to make an observation and I mention it with the greatest respect to all who wear the *sheitel*.

I believe that people should be aware that the woman covering her hair is observing the tradition of *tzniut* (modesty). Quite some decades ago, the wig was not very developed and it was clear that it was not the wearer's natural hair. This projected a signal that an Orthodox Jewish woman was wearing it as a symbol of modesty. Today, the wig has become so sophisticated that it is actually more alluring than the person's natural hair. Beautiful wigs are being worn universally, including movie stars and society ladies. It seems impossible to be able to differentiate between natural hair and a wig.

The truth of the matter is that there are various ways in which a woman can observe *tzniut* (modesty) and it would depend upon her family, education and social circle. Whichever path she chooses will undoubtedly bring blessing upon her and her family.

A Taste of Responsa

Responsa is a unique category of Jewish literature that addresses questions posed by people of all classes to the most eminent Talmudic authorities at any given period. The questions span every aspect of life and are utilized as references, as well as sources for study.

The following are selected samples of this fascinating branch of Jewish literature.

Are *Tefillin* Allowed?

A man was about to be admitted to a hospital which specialized in highly communicable diseases. Anyone who entered the hospital had to sign a legal agreement that all personal effects brought into the hospital could not be removed upon discharge. In fact, they had to be burned.

An observant Jewish man was faced with a dilemma. He was accepted as a patient in the hospital and planned to bring his *tefillin* (phylacteries) with him. After all, except for Shabbat and holidays, he prayed with them on a daily basis and would be devastated if he could not do so during his confinement. But if he brought them, he would be legally committed to having them destroyed by fire upon his release. This would certainly be a great desecration of these holy items. On the other hand, if he were to leave them at home, he would not be able to perform the *mitzva* (commandment) of praying with them every day, as he had done throughout his life.

What to do?

The question was posed to Rabbi Moshe Feinstein. In his response *(Igrot Moshe - Orach Chaim: siman 2),* the rabbi pointed out that since it

123

was a certainty that the *tefillin* would be destroyed, it was forbidden for him to bring them into the hospital. The daily *mitzva* of praying with the *tefillin* would have to be waived until his discharge. The man could take comfort in the fact that he was prevented from wearing the *tefillin* because of his desire to protect their sanctity.

May One Not Fasting on Yom Kippur Get an Aliya?

Rabbi Ezekiel Landau, known as the *Nodah B'Yehuda* (1713-1793) was asked the following question:

An ailing person was told by his doctor that it was required of him to eat some food with his medicine which he had to take on Yom Kippur. During the service, the man was offered an *Aliya* ("called up" to the Torah). Since he had broken the fast by eating some food with his medicine, he was reluctant to accept this honor.

How should he respond?

In his book of Responsa, there is no recorded answer offered by the rabbi! Perhaps the answer was lost somehow over the years.

In the most humble manner, I would venture a possible solution. Since this man ate something in response to a doctor's order, the refusal of which would have endangered his life, it was really not his choice. He was simply following halachic norms.

As a result, he could accept the *Aliya*.

Who Precedes in Marriage?

A young man came home with the good news that he had proposed marriage to a woman and she had accepted. Coming from a very observant family, he wanted the wedding to take place as soon as possible. His older brother strenuously protested, claiming that it was his right to be the first to marry.

Who precedes? Should the younger brother be asked to wait a reasonable period of time in the interest of *shalom bayit* (keeping peace in the home) or should the younger brother be allowed to perform the *mitzva* of marriage and procreation immediately despite his brother?

Rabbi Moshe Feinstein (*Igrot Moshe - Even Ha'ezer: Part II, siman aleph*), ruled as follows:

Since the younger brother had reached the age of maturity and matrimony, there is no justification to make him and his bride wait for an undetermined period of time.

Only if the two brothers were to be married at the same time should the older brother precede the younger.

The Case of the Blocked Car

A man returned to his parked car in a congested Israeli neighborhood. To his chagrin, he saw that his car was surrounded by parked taxis. The area was apparently a taxi headquarters and he asked the drivers to please move their taxis to enable him to leave. They informed him that they were having lunch and would move their cars in due time. Extremely incensed, the man made five calls to the taxi company, requesting their service in five different locations. The drivers immediately drove off in their cars.

When the taxi company somehow discovered the ruse, they went to a *beit din* (Jewish court of law) and demanded restitution from the man for the lost fares.

The Dilemma: Since the man never intended to hire the taxis, must he pay a certain amount to compensate for the five fares? On the other hand, is the taxi company responsible for its loss because their drivers blocked the man's path?

The Response: In *Shulchan Aruch, Choshen Mishpat* (42 2:2), it states: "If one covered a street with jars, thereby preventing passage … if a passerby smashed them in order to pass, he is not responsible to pay for them."

It would thus seem that the man is not obligated to pay for the fares he ordered to clear the road.

Leave the Hospital to Hear the *Shofar*?

A mentally disturbed patient who was hospitalized was pronounced cured, but the doctors recommended he remain a few weeks to strengthen the cure.

Question: Should he leave the hospital to hear the *shofar* on Rosh Hashana?

Dilemma: Hearing the *shofar* is a Torah commandment and he has been declared essentially cured. On the other hand, since he is still gaining mental strength, his premature presence in society could cause a relapse.

Response: He should not leave the hospital at this point in his recovery because of the danger of a relapse. *(Igrot Moshe - Volume I, page 293)*

Moving the Torah for One Reading

A Torah should not be moved from its regular place unless it will be read at least three times in its new locale.

Question: The family of a *chatan* (bridegroom) requested a Torah from a synagogue to be brought into their home for the *Aufruf*. There were many people who were to receive *aliyot*.

Dilemma: Allowing the Torah to be moved for only one reading would be a breach of tradition. Reading the Torah in *shul* would be a burden on the congregation when many people would be "called up."

Response: Rabbi Moshe Feinstein allowed the removal of the Torah to the place of the *Aufruf. (Igrot Moshe - Volume 1, Page 143)*. He based his reply on the fact that, although not all *poskim* (decisors) agree, Torah scrolls are moved to different locations for Simchat Torah readings. An *Aufruf* is also a great *Simcha* (joyous occasion). And furthermore, a bridegroom is compared to a king, thereby making him worthy of this honor.

Marriage on Condition of No Children

Background: The Jewish concept of marriage is for the purpose of procreation and companionship.

Question: A man stated that for reasons of health, he is not mentally and emotionally able to bring up children. May he marry a woman on the condition that they will not have children?

Dilemma: If he will not be allowed to marry under those conditions, he will be forced to live alone, which is not considered the optimum halachic condition. If he will marry a woman with this exclusion, he may be the cause of an improper birth control.

Response: Rabbi Moshe Feinstein ruled that the man may not marry under this condition. Such exclusions can only be imposed because of the woman – if, for example, the pregnancy could present a danger to her – even the possibility of suffering severe pain. However, no prohibitive dangers would apply to the man, such as the raising of children.

*   *   *

Besides the great degree of interest these Responsa generate, it is important to understand the crucial role they have played in the development of Halacha (Jewish law) throughout the generations. There are constant new developments, such as electricity, new forms of transportation and the whole realm of medical ethics, to cite just a few. The greatest Jewish minds of each generation ponder these new challenges in terms of the continuation of Torah law. It is an ongoing process assuring contemporary relevance of all aspects of Jewish life.

The Hidden Matza

*M*atza, or unleavened bread, enjoys universal prominence. It is the symbol of the Exodus of the Jewish people from their Egyptian slavery. After living in a crushing servitude for a period of two hundred and ten years, their departure came at a moment's notice. Having no time to prepare bread for the coming day, they threw sacks of dough over their shoulders and headed into the desert, where they ultimately baked the dough in the glare and heat of the sun. Thus, the *matza* was born.

This basic bread is also known as the "bread of affliction" or the "bread of poverty." Every people has its unique bread. The Jewish people also enjoy challah and bagels. However, *matza* is bread without any frills. It represents the basic needs of man.

Needless to state, the *matza* plays a pivotal role at the *Seder* on Pesach. At one point at this annual ceremony, however, it assumes a somewhat different role. It becomes the *Afikomen*. In the time of the Holy Temple, the *Seder* concluded with the eating of the *Korban Pesach,* the Paschal Lamb. With the destruction of the Holy Temple, the lamb could no longer be sacrificed and the *Afikomen* took its place. With everyone at the *Seder* partaking of a piece, all eating ceased for the evening.

I would like to end by describing a little custom in my family, although I have heard it practiced by others. A piece of the *Afikomen* is placed in its bag and put aside. The following year, when the *chametz* is burned before Passover, this piece of the "hidden *matza*" is placed with the *chametz* and burned. I have never discovered the reason for this *minhag* (custom), but it is a nice feeling which somehow fuses the past and the future together.

Jewish Humor

"Worship God in joy." (Psalms 100:2)

Perhaps the above verse from Psalms is one of the reasons the Jewish people find joy and humor in every aspect of life. I have always opted for a cheerful approach to the rabbinate, religion and, for that matter, to life itself.

There are far too many who find no place in religion for humor. To them, it is all a very somber business. What is there to laugh about? Religion demands constant and serious attention from birth to death. Any deviation must be frowned upon. These folks are making a sad mistake. The truth of the matter is that humor and good cheer have always been part and parcel of Jewish culture. Did you ever try to tell a **new** Jewish joke?

I do not believe that any ethnic group has laughed as much at itself as the Jewish people. Actually, we cry almost as much. Consider a Jewish wedding. Half the guests are either sobbing openly or heroically suppressing their tears. Or, for that matter, friends of the deceased manage to gather in a discreet corner at a funeral to exchange humorous stories about their dear departed.

Do we find humor in the Torah and in our books of Jewish learning? Perhaps there is more than we realize. But we have to look between the lines. Did you ever consider that the Almighty might have created His world with just a touch of irony – perhaps even with a hint of wit for those sensitive enough to catch it? Just think about the "rib-tickling" implications of Eve being created from the rib of Adam. The story goes that Adam came home late one night and the first thing Eve did was to count his ribs!

In the book of *Bemidbar* (Numbers), there is the story of a donkey actually speaking to his master, Balaam. Just picture the scene. Along the way, an angel wanted to kill Balaam. Somehow, the donkey sensed the danger and refused to continue walking. Balaam, who saw nothing, was infuriated and began to beat the hapless animal. Suddenly, the donkey began to speak and gave Balaam a lecture he would never forget.

We all know that it took the Children of Israel no less than forty years to arrive at the Promised Land. This circuitous route seemed a real puzzle to a man who was discussing the weekly Torah portion with his friend.

"Why," he wondered, "do you think Moses led them through such remote areas in the wilderness?"

"That's easy," his friend rejoined. "The way they were carrying on, he was embarrassed to take them through the populated areas."

There is also the story of an author who announced that he was going to write a book about humor in the Talmud. Try as he might, he simply could not find any outright jokes. As he was about to give up, he chanced upon a Talmudic passage which read, "Torah scholars increase peace in the world." With all the "branches" of Judaism and their attendant controversies, with innumerable religious leaders vying with each other for followers, the author could not stop laughing. It was the best joke he had ever heard.

Coming to more modern times, we manage to laugh even in the face of death. This story concerns a father who had come to the local Hebrew school to pick up his son. Being a few minutes early, he sauntered into the hall and stopped in front of his son's classroom. He was shocked as he heard the teacher patiently and repeatedly prompt his son.

"Yitgadal V'Yitkadash ..."

Aware of the fact that this was the memorial prayer recited by children for deceased parents, the father stormed into the classroom and confronted the teacher. "Rabbi," he fumed, "I am still a comparatively young man. Is that the only thing you can teach my son?"

The rabbi looked at him with sad eyes and replied, "My friend, I want to bestow a blessing upon you. You should live so long until he gets it right!"

I can think of no better way to close this essay than to quote the famous saying of Rabbi Nachman of Breslov: "It is a great *mitzva* to always be in a state joy."

TORAH AND TALMUDIC INSIGHTS

Scripture states that Adam was created from the dust of the earth. Which part of the earth? From every sector, to prevent any man from saying, "The world was created for my sake." (Sanhedrin 38b)

***

Rabbi Yochanan Ben Zakkai said, "If you have a sapling in your hand and are told, 'Look the Messiah is coming,' you should first plant the sapling and then go on to welcome the Messiah." (Avot de'Rabbi Natan 31)

The Garden of Eden Exists

It is a common misconception that when Adam and Eve sinned and were driven out of the Garden of Eden, the garden was destroyed. A simple reading of the biblical text will quickly disclose this error.

> And He drove Adam out and stationed at the east of the Garden of Eden the *Cherubim* and the flame of the ever-turning sword, to guard the way to the Tree of Life. (Genesis 3:24)

Had we been informed that the Garden was destroyed after the expulsion, there would never have been the possibility of a return. It thus seems clear that there was a future plan for the Garden. It was never intended to be permanently destroyed.

Was the Garden of Eden just a specific parcel of land or does it perhaps represent the lofty and spiritual existence which was intended by God for mankind which was aborted due to the sins of Adam and Eve? The fact that the Torah is very clear about its continued existence should be a great consolation and challenge for each and every one of us. True, the return to Eden is guarded and may not allow easy access. Nevertheless, it exists and beckons us to constantly attempt to return. Mankind was obviously meant to live a peaceful and lofty existence. The fact that Eden was abandoned at a very early stage of history could well have been only a temporary suspension.

If mankind's actions will one day finally vindicate God's intentions at the time of creation, the *Cherubim* will lift their fiery swords and beckon mankind to reenter the Garden of Eden.

What was the First Sin?

When the average person is asked to identify the first sin recorded in the Torah, he will invariably respond that it was Eve eating from the Tree of Knowledge in direct violation of the command of God. However, if one reads the verses a little more carefully, it will become obvious that this response is not quite correct. The above was, in fact, the second sin.

Let us examine the texts.

> And God commanded Adam, "You may eat freely of every tree in the Garden, but of the Tree of Knowledge of good and evil, you shall not **eat**." (Genesis 2:16-17)

And later.

The woman (Eve) said to the serpent, "We may eat of the fruit of the trees in the Garden, but God said, 'You shall not eat of the fruit of the tree that is in the middle of the Garden, **nor shall you touch it'**" (Genesis 3:11).

The difference between the two versions becomes immediately apparent. In no way or manner did God forbid Adam and Eve to touch the Tree. It was an embellishment by Eve. In fact, there are commentaries who point to this exaggeration as the cause of the sin. They quote the Midrash that the serpent took Eve's hand and touched the Tree. When nothing happened to her, the serpent cleverly claimed that the entire warning by God was meaningless and she had nothing to fear.

Thus, it is clear to me that the first sin in this entire situation was Eve's attempt to be more scrupulous than God required and this was the direct cause for the ensuing sin and the consequent banishment of Adam and Eve from the Garden of Eden.

What Eve was doing is something that has been emulated by Jewish people and, I am sure, by others from time immemorial. It is the urge to outdo that which is required. The Jewish people have always been warned to overcome this tendency. We are to seek the *Shevil Hazahav*, the Golden Path, which is the Middle of the Road, as elaborated by the Rambam (Moses Maimonides) in *The Eight Chapters*.

There is no limit to the examples of those who insist on going further than what is reasonably expected. To give one example, I refer to the Glatt kosher meals which are served on the Israeli El Al planes. Yet invariably, there are those who will order some form of "super Glatt." I doubt that they have any complaint against the basic food which is served. It is simply unacceptable for them to be part of the regular crowd, no matter what the conditions may be. Other illustrations are legion.

This insistence is not always a matter of harmless upmanship. Sometimes it may bear dire consequences. I refer, for example, to a Jewish community wherein one rather large market refused to deal with meats and poultry of universally accepted *kashrut* agencies. They insisted on using their own sources of supply. Their rabbi had total trust in the reliability of the *mashgiach* (religious overseer). If I am not mistaken, the rabbi was warned a number of times that there were questionable activities going on in that huge establishment, but he was so sure of the system that he simply ignored them.

It was ultimately discovered that for a number of years, the source of the meat and poultry being sold was totally non-kosher. It was not a question of simply being a problematic source - it was outright *treiff* (non-kosher). The incident rocked the kosher world and it was another example of how making oneself more religious than required can bring dire consequences in its wake.

As I see it, the sin of Eve in being sanctimoniously more observant than requested by God should serve as a lesson for each and every one of us. Certainly, we should not do less than we are commanded, but it is equally erroneous to veer off the "Golden Path" by engaging in activities which are beyond the requirements, especially if the motive is to make oneself look more pious in the eyes of others.

Only One Commandment

The following thoughts are based upon a Torah commentary by Rabbi Samson Raphael Hirsch (1808-1888). Besides the divine imperative of having children, the only *mitzva* (commandment) which was given to Adam and Eve was to refrain from eating the fruit of the Tree of Knowledge.

There is certainly no dearth of ethical or spiritual norms by which Adam and Eve could have been commanded to live. Perhaps to love one's neighbor as oneself, to walk humbly upon the earth or to worship God and spend time studying about His essence and nature. Or, a combination of many of these commands. Yet, of all these possibilities, the single commandment which they were directed to obey was a food restriction - to refrain from eating fruit from the Tree of Knowledge!

Upon reflection, however, this was not such a simple or trivial command. Physical sustenance, which comes about through eating, touches upon the very core of man's being. When the infant leaves the warmth and contentment of its mother's womb, it screams in terror until the nurturing milk stills its cries. The infant never forgets that first pleasurable moment and continues to satiate itself with food and new culinary sensations throughout life.

It thus becomes clear that God commanded a discipline in the most intimate realm of human experience. Perhaps the many and complex rules and regulations of *kashrut* (Jewish dietary laws) stem from this original commandment.

Throughout Jewish history, the treatment of food has played a crucial role both in the individual and communal life of the people. There are many who would relegate all the religious and spiritual dietary laws to matters of hygiene. Those who proclaim the health aspect of these regulations to be obsolete have simply discarded them. They refuse to ascribe any spiritual or disciplinary values to their observance. Sadly, they have totally missed the point.

On the other hand, those who seek to increase their highest level of spirituality via the laws pertaining to food have also selected this area of observance to an exceptionally intense degree. Thus, we find many levels of *kashrut*, with different groups vying with each other for more extreme forms of observance. On Passover, many subscribe to the strict prohibition of eating unleavened bread or its products which came into contact with moisture even after having been baked. In matters of meat, the well-known *Glatt* requirement continues to gain popularity from year to year. In fact, this designation is now improperly applied to many foods other than meat. The concept among these people seems to be that the greater the stringency in matters of food, whether applicable or not, the higher the level of religiosity.

It should be clear that there is much more to the Jewish dietary laws than a mere adjustment of menu. Those who discarded these regulations as physical rituals to be totally abandoned in modern times are in great error. On the most basic level, these rules may contain benefits to one's health that we have not as yet even begun to fathom. Furthermore, they have unified the Jewish people on the deepest sociological levels. But there are more profound concepts underlying the laws of *kashrut* of which we may still be totally ignorant.

It is crucial to observe these ancient dietary laws in the spirit in which they were given, dating back to the commandment which was conveyed to Adam and Eve. On the one hand, they must be carefully maintained and not rejected as was done by the first human beings. On the other hand, their observance must be within the parameters of their intent and not be magnified as Eve attempted by claiming that the Tree may not be touched which was not included in the commandment. Over-zealousness can be as injurious as lack of observance. It is good to always remember that the *Shvil Hazahav*, the Golden Road, is the path of logic and reason.

"And God Blessed Abraham With Everything" (Genesis 24:1)

Everything?

Let us consider some of the events in his life.

- He was terribly persecuted by Nimrod.
- At the age of seventy-five, he had to leave his home – to an unknown destination.
- He went through the agony of the *Akedah,* almost sacrificing his beloved son, Isaac.
- His nephew, Lot, was kidnapped and he recruited an army of 318 soldiers to rescue him.
- He prayed for the survival of the cities of Sodom and Gomorrah and had to witness their destruction.
- He had to banish Hagar and his son Yishmael from his home, which greatly distressed him.
- He had to resort to the ploy of claiming that Sarah was his sister and came close to suffering dangerous consequences.

And on and on ...

All of the above can lead one to wonder at the words of the Torah that God had blessed Abraham with **everything**!

A parallel to this seemingly difficult assessment may be found in the following story.

A very wealthy man was constantly suffering from depression. He never felt that he had enough and he tended to be envious of those who enjoyed greater prosperity. In an effort to overcome these feelings, he visited his rabbi to seek some advice.

The rabbi listened closely to what he had to say and then told him to visit a man in the most poverty stricken part of the city. This came as somewhat of a surprise to the rich person, who expected to be sent to another man of means, a doctor or someone of reasonable importance. But, of course, he had great respect for the rabbi and wound his way through rubble and dirt to the address of the man he had been instructed to visit.

When the door was opened for him, he could not believe his eyes. Seldom had he encountered such poverty. Greeting him from behind a broken table, a bent over man asked him to sit in a torn and shoddy sofa. The man's hair was long and straggly and his entire face was covered with pocks.

"Welcome," the man greeted him. "What brings you here?"

With great difficulty, the wealthy man explained that he came at the rabbi's instructions. "I suppose he sent me here to see all this poverty and misery to show me how much better off I am."

"Oh, no," the poor man insisted. "There must be some mistake. I'm sure the rabbi sent you to the wrong address. You see, I am more than satisfied with everything God has given me. I consider this to be a warm and comfortable home and the little physical problems I have really don't amount to much. No one could be happier and more satisfied than myself."

The wealthy man left the house in a daze. He could not believe what he had seen and heard. Never again did he complain.

Yes, God truly blessed Abraham with everything.

Perhaps, if we ever become dissatisfied or envious of others, it would be a good idea to measure our lives in terms of the man described above.

The Goal is Cloaked in Mystery

If Abraham would have had a GPS in his time, he would have had a problem setting it. Not once, but twice, is our forefather commanded by God to set out on a journey and in both cases, he did not receive any knowledge as to what his destination was to be.

Let us review the first case.

> And God said to Abram, "Go from your country and your birthplace and your father's home **to the land that I will show you**." (Genesis 12:1)

Note that while it was made abundantly clear from where Abraham was *beginning* his journey, the *destination* was not revealed to him. In which direction should he set out? How could he even take his first step?

There is a second such instance. I refer to the chapter known as the *Akedah* ("The Binding of Isaac").

Following is the text:

> And it was after these events that God tested Abraham. And He said to him, "Abraham!" And he said, "Here I am." And He said, "Take your son, your only son whom you love, Isaac, and go to the region of Moriah and sacrifice him there as a burnt offering **on a mountain that I will show you**." (Genesis 22:1-2)

How very strange! In both cases, the destination was withheld from Abraham.

Passing over some of the explanations given by the classical commentaries, I would venture an opinion of my own. While we may set out on a host of journeys, there is absolutely no guarantee as to the outcome. In fact, this is the rule of our very lives. Perhaps there is an unrevealed road which has been determined for us, culminating in a specific destination.

This concept is borne out by the teaching that when our journey on earth has been completed and we stand before the ultimate Tribunal, we will never be asked, "Why were you not like Abraham or Moses?" or "Why did you not live up to the standards of Sarah or Miriam?" The only questions we will be asked is, "Did you arrive at your determined destination?" In other words, did we achieve the destinations which were within our means?

Abraham was to begin a new life in another land – Canaan. The whole project was up to him – how he would get there, what he would do upon his arrival, etc. That is the essence of free choice. It may seem difficult to comprehend, but God did not even give him the direction in which to travel. The Torah makes it quite clear that Abraham sensed the correct path that his journey was to take. We know that he succeeded greatly in all his undertakings.

The same scenario played out when he was faced with many mountains on his way to the *Akedah.* He looked at them and somehow he knew. Then he and his beloved son, Isaac, reached their intended destination, Mount Moriah, and together they enacted one of the greatest dramas in human history.

Herein lies the secret of all our lives. We know where we are at the moment, but we do not know where even the next moment will lead us. Armed with our faith in God to prevent us from going astray, we approach each mountain and make every effort to reach the top by ascending from strength to strength.

"Little" Isaac

Throughout the ages, one of the major sources and inspiration of art has been the Bible. However, some of these biblical sources have been so misunderstood that, at times, the artwork produced a totally distorted result. An example of this phenomenon would be Michelangelo's statue of Moses. The striking aspect of this sculpture is the two horns emanating from Moses' head.

How could this be?

To understand how this colossal mistake came about, we must turn to the event in the Bible whose content was misread. Moses had been atop Mount Sinai for a period of forty days. He had been exposed to an intensive divine radiance during this period. When he descended, we read that he did not know that his face was shining (*karan*) – that a radiance emanated from his face. People were very uneasy about this strange sight and kept their distance, as a result of which Moses placed a veil over his face.

Judging from the outcome, it appears quite clear that the sculptor's advisor was not much of a biblical scholar. The words in the Torah are without vowels. Thus, *karan* (radiance) could just as well have been read as *keren* (horn), since the consonants are the same. Of course, the correct reading would depend upon the context, which was not taken into consideration.

The same erroneous conclusions hold true of "little Isaac." Here we are not dealing with a mistranslation, but with faulty calculations. The famous event of the *Akedah* (Binding of Isaac) is immortalized through many masterpiece paintings. They invariably depict Abraham, in the very prime of his life, leading a little boy to a pile of wood, which was to serve as the altar.

Not so! A careful reading of the biblical texts will quickly determine that Abraham was no less than 137 years old, while his son, Isaac, in the prime of his life, was 37 years old.

All the artwork depicting that immortal scene would have been quite different if the facts had been correctly ascertained. We would have seen an aged man leading a much younger and robust son - exactly the opposite of the depictions!

Regardless, the spiritual message is even stronger when one realizes that Isaac could have easily pushed aside his old and much weaker father and run away. Yet, the Torah teaches, "And the two walked together" (Genesis 22:6). The closeness of the generations is one of the cornerstones of the Jewish faith.

Where Was Sarah?

Every indication in the Torah points to the fact that Abraham and Sarah enjoyed a deep and loving relationship. When the three visitors/angels appeared, both worked together to prepare a sumptuous meal for them. When Ishmael presented a problem to the upbringing of Isaac, God told Abraham to listen to Sarah's instructions. Wherever they traveled, Sarah and Abraham did so together.

All of which creates a perplexing problem. When Abraham was called upon by God to take his son, Isaac, to the mountain to be offered as a sacrifice, Sarah is nowhere to be seen or heard. She was probably in a different place when the two headed out, but Abraham made no move to inform her of what was happening or to ask her to accompany them. Since this in no way conforms to the usual relationship which they shared, one wonders how the conditions in this circumstance were different.

The answer which I would like to propose is that God expects of us only that with which we can cope. For example, we may only fast on Yom Kippur if our health permits. Citing another illustration, it is proper to give charity only to the point that the family budget is not endangered. There are many such examples in every phase of life.

One can only imagine how hard it was for Abraham to take his beloved son to a place where he thought he would have to sacrifice him. Yet somehow he forced himself to carry out God's bidding and continued with his mission. Difficult as it was, God apparently expected Abraham to cope with this command. However, and herein lies my point, to request a Jewish mother to sacrifice her child, even as a divine imperative, is simply beyond the pale of human capability. God only commanded Abraham and did not include Sarah. Abraham must have understood this and, as a result, withheld the entire matter from her. In fact, the Midrash deduces from the Torah reading that shortly after becoming aware of this episode, Sarah died.

I believe that herein lies a lesson for every one of us. There are times when carrying out the dictates of Halacha (Jewish law) creates serious difficulties and places a heavy burden upon us. But this fact, in and of itself, should not deter us from doing that which is required. If it is something beyond our capability, we are absolved from the task. Difficult, however, is not impossible and it is important that we always be aware of the difference.

The House of Israel

It seems that as long as one can remember, the collective Jewish people have been referred to as the House of Israel. This term is employed in the Bible, prayers and virtually all of Jewish literature. Yet, one wonders about the origin of this word. After all, "house" connotes dwelling, not the collective sum of a people.

I have given this matter quite some thought and research. Finally, an idea occurred to me which I can only substantiate on logic. Unfortunately, I do not have any hard evidence or proof.

The Torah is replete with examples of sibling rivalry. I refer to Cain and Abel, Jacob and Esau, as well as the dysfunctional family of Joseph and his brothers.

The relationship between Aaron, Miriam and Moses was always described on a loving and familial level. However, an incident occurred in the book of Numbers that I believe is the source of this appellation. It describes how Aaron and Miriam criticized their brother for having married an Ethiopian woman. The commentaries spend a great deal of time analyzing their complaint, but this is not the subject on which I am focusing. The reaction of Moses apparently was total silence. It seems that his great humility prevented him from lashing back, which would have been the expected response of most siblings. As it turned out, God Himself came to Moses' defense, after which Miriam contracted leprosy, which was cured by Moses' intervening prayer on her behalf.

The following are the words which God addressed to Aaron and Miriam:

"Not so My servant Moses; in My entire *house* he is the trusted one" (Numbers 12:7).

From this verse it would seem that God looked upon Israel as His house. Perhaps there is more to this allusion than meets the eye. It might indicate that just as a house has many rooms with varying functions, so can the Jewish people be categorized into many sections, although always remaining one unit under one roof, as it were.

Perhaps this is the source and the meaning of the term which characterizes the Jewish people throughout the ages as the House of Israel.

Rebecca Revisited

The story in Genesis is well-known in which Eliezer, Abraham's servant, sets out on a journey to seek a wife for his master's son, Isaac. He devised a stratagem whereby a compassionate woman would offer him water. As we know, Rebecca came forward and not only offered him water, but supplied drinks for all his camels – a huge undertaking. Eliezer accepted her kindheartedness and Rebecca soon left her home to become Isaac's wife.

To me, this heart-warming incident came full circle during a visit to Israel when my daughter, Shira, drove to a mini-mall with me to shop in one of the stores. It was a hot day in May and the area of which I speak was very close to where the incident with Eliezer and Rebecca took place.

I was well aware of the fact that when women do their shopping, especially for clothing, one must be ready to wait a long time, something that I was prepared to do. I looked for a ledge on which to sit when Shira came out of the store carrying a folding chair. I had no idea if she asked to borrow it or simply took it out. I was more than happy to take advantage of the offer to sit and bask in the hot sun.

It did not take long for a woman, who was obviously working in the store, to come out. She looked straight in my direction and began to walk toward me quite purposefully. This was not good, I said to myself. It must be the chair. Shira probably took it out without permission and I was going to be seriously chastised for this unauthorized act.

I was more than relieved to see that the young woman had a smile on her face when she reached me, but that was not all. In her hand, she held a cup. She told me that she saw me sitting in the hot sun and insisted that I drink some cold water.

I am sure I had never seen her before, nor did she know me. I was almost too dumbfounded for words, but I managed a sincere, "*Toda* (thank you)."

To me, this was a reenactment of a biblical scene. Its warmth and friendship spoke volumes. This was the real Israel.

I cannot help but wonder if her name was Rebecca.

"And the Boys Grew"

The above words are found in Genesis (25:27) and refer to the growth of the two brothers, Jacob and Esau, into manhood. We believe that no words are wasted in the Torah and every word must have a reason. That having been said, the question immediately rises as to the need for stating that the boys grew, prior to describing what their avocations were to be. Of course they had to first grow! Was that phrase really necessary?

As is well known, although they were twins, Jacob and Esau grew into very different adults. The former continued the family traditions, while Esau, on the other hand, became a hunter with a very coarse and violent personality.

It is quite possible that the phrase "and the boys grew" carries an implicit complaint against the parents. It appears that their early growth seemed unimportant. Isaac and Rebecca did not become actively engaged until their children had become young adults. At that point, the die had already been cast. It turned out that the difference in their personalities was enormous.

A simple story which can act as a strong analogy is that of a father who brought his five year old son to the rabbi. "When do you think I should start his Jewish education?" the father wanted to know. The rabbi took a moment and replied, "I think you had better hurry. You see, you are already five years late!"

There is no guarantee in the upbringing and training of children. This, however, does not release parents from their responsibility of closely watching their children's progress from earliest infancy. Who knows? Had this been done with Jacob and Esau, their relationship might have been much closer and history might have continued in a very different direction.

Who is This "Ish"?

There are two instances in the Torah which speak of a mystical being who is simply referred to as an "*ish*." The translation of this word is "man," but that helps little in defining who this being may be.

Let me explain.

Our first meeting in the Torah with this *ish* is when Jacob, prior to the reunion with his brother, Esau, was all alone at night.

> And Jacob was left alone and an *ish* (man) wrestled with him until the dawn... And the *ish* said, "Let me go for the dawn is rising" and (Jacob) said, "I will not let you go until you bless me." And he said, "What is your name?" And he answered, "Jacob." And he said, "No longer shall your name be Jacob, but rather Israel." (Genesis 32:25-27)

It is interesting that in this crucial engagement, the being that was wrestling with Jacob did not identify himself, although it was clear that he had supernatural powers, such as changing Jacob's name to Israel.

Before attempting to analyze this apparition's role, let us see where he appears the second time.

We fast forward to Joseph carrying out his father's wishes to find his brothers tending their sheep and bringing a report regarding their welfare.

> And he (Joseph) found an *ish* ... and the *ish* asked him, saying, "What are you seeking?" And he responded, "I

am seeking my brothers. Please tell me where they are pasturing." (Genesis 37:15-16)

Except for the fact that this *ish* informed Joseph as to his brothers' whereabouts, we are told nothing further about him.

There are glaring questions. Why was the *ish* there precisely at the moment that Joseph was passing by? How did he know who Joseph's brothers were? How did he know exactly where his brothers were feeding their flocks?

So the question remains. Who was this *ish* who tried to harm Jacob and sent Joseph into the hands of his violent and envious brothers?

There is a common denominator to both instances. The original intent of the *ish* was to cause harm to both Jacob and Joseph. In the first instance, he wrestled with Jacob and, in fact, did harm him. He struck him in the thigh, forcing Jacob to leave the encounter limping. It is for this reason, the Torah tells us, that we are not allowed to eat the *gid hanashe* (sciatic nerve) of an animal.

Most important, however, is the fact that after Jacob sustained the suffering of the blow to his body, his stature was elevated. Instead of continuing to be called Jacob (from the word "heel"), his name was changed by being elevated to Israel, meaning to have struggled with man and God and prevailed. I personally also perceive in the Hebrew name *Yisrael* that of *yashar kayl*, which means "straightforward with God."

A similar scenario transpired in the case of Joseph. The *ish* sent him into a perilous situation which could well have resulted in his death. He was navigated right into the hands of his angry and jealous brothers who were about to kill him. It was only a change of plans which made them decide to throw him into a pit and ultimately sell him into Egyptian slavery.

But, again, there was a most fascinating twist in the story. Although Joseph was grievously hurt at the outset, his condition dramatically changed to the point that he eventually became the viceroy of Egypt!

These two incidents, beginning in suffering and rising to a much greater and positive development were commented upon by Rabbi Joseph B. Soloveitchik (1903-1993) in a manner that I have always remembered.

Throughout history, Rabbi Soloveitchik explained, there is a mystical *ish* who, in one way or another, causes great initial suffering to our people. Regardless of the initial pain, however, the Jewish people have invariably not only survived the original catastrophe, but have invariably risen to greater heights.

Far too many pages would have to be written to demonstrate the truth of this principle from the time of the first Egyptian oppression to this very day. I will simply choose the most recent and perhaps devastating of them all - the *Shoah* - which caused our people to limp as did Jacob and even threatened our very future.

Yet, miraculously, from the ashes of this unspeakable tragedy, the State of Israel was born and is growing in every way. Again, the *ish* caused devastation but, far from succeeding, our people rose to much greater heights.

It is very mystical and very puzzling, but it is a reality.

It would seem that we are now looking to the ultimate meeting with the *ish*, which will result in our final Redemption. It is our hope and prayer that the genesis of this greatest of ages will not be preceded by any disasters.

A Positive Ending?

All those who have ever been in charge of the public Torah reading know that it is important that each reading concludes on a positive note. Of course, this was all prepared years ago, when those who arranged the Torah portions saw to it that they ended on the correct themes. Sometimes, arrangements have to be made when more than seven men are called to the Torah on a Shabbat morning because of a *Simcha* or other special occasion. The rule is always the same – the conclusion of the current reading must end on an affirmative theme.

That having been established, there is one weekly Torah reading whose ending seems to fly into the face of this rule. I refer to the end of the Torah portion of *Vayeshev* (Genesis: Chapters 37-40).

A synopsis of the events finds Joseph in jail where he had been unjustly thrown because of false charges against him by Potiphar's wife. One day, Pharaoh's Chief Butler and Head Baker were jailed. Joseph noticed that they were depressed and he asked them for the reason. Both had a dream which disturbed them greatly and Joseph offered to interpret the dreams for them. It turned out that within three days, the baker was to be hanged and the butler was pardoned and returned to his position as Pharaoh's Cup Bearer. Joseph asked the Cup Bearer to intervene for him to Pharaoh because he was innocent of the charges which had been brought against him.

It is at this point that the weekly Torah reading ends with the following words.

"And the Chief Butler did not remember Joseph and forgot him." (Genesis 40:23)

What a seemingly negative ending. Not only did the Chief Butler fail to remember Joseph, but he forgot him!

And so, Joseph was left to linger in prison.

This apparently unhappy conclusion of a Torah section seems to be contrary to everything that has been taught on the matter.

But all is not always what it seems.

We learn in a Mishna in the Tractate of *Brachot* (Chapter 9, Mishna 5):

"A person is obligated to bless God upon evil as he would bless upon good."

I believe that the message of this Mishna is that there is no pure unadulterated evil. Even in what appears to us as bad, there is some element of good - perhaps not visible upon the surface. It would be difficult to have to bless something which is totally evil.

Could it be possible, then, that the conclusion of *Vayeshev* is not all negative - not intrinsically evil?

Let us assume that the Chief Butler would have remembered Joseph. Pharaoh might have commuted his sentence **at that time**. Joseph would have left by the back door and returned to his home in disgrace. His brothers may have turned on him and on each other and it is hard to guess what their father would have done. Jewish history would hardly have progressed as it did.

As it turned out, Joseph remained in prison for two more years, interpreted the dreams of Pharaoh and became viceroy of Egypt!

So we see that upon some reflection, the Torah portion of *Vayeshev* actually ended on a note of blessing - even if somewhat delayed.

I believe that there is a deep lesson in this for each and every one of us. When matters seem very bad, perhaps a deeper look will reveal many rays of light. Everything contains the seeds of blessing.

The Grave by The Wayside

The love which Jacob felt for his wife, Rachel, is beautifully recounted in the Bible. We learn that as the family was travelling past Bethlehem, Rachel died while giving birth to her son, Benjamin. We read that Jacob buried her by the wayside - right on the side of the road! What seems most unbelievable is that Jacob did not wait to bury her in the family plot in Hebron, which was a very short distance ahead. Was this the proper respect to be shown to his beloved wife?

The answer came many centuries later. In the year 70 C.E., the Babylonians had destroyed Jerusalem and the Holy Temple. Thousands were taken captive and were being exiled from Israel. The road upon which they were led brought them past Rachel's grave.

The prophet Jeremiah describes what happened:

> A voice is heard, mourning and great weeping. Rachel is crying for her children and refusing to be comforted. And God says, "Restrain your voice from weeping and your eyes from tears. For your efforts will be rewarded and they will return from the land of the enemy." (Jeremiah 31:14)

And seventy years later, the exiles returned on the same route, past Rachel's grave.

What a powerful story! Somehow Rachel did not give even God peace until her children came home.

No wonder it is such a holy site today. There are countless stories of prayers having been answered and of numerous women who were rewarded with babies after their sincere supplications to Mother Rachel to intervene on their behalf. People from all walks of life gather there on a daily basis and it is fascinating to note how friendly all these contrasting types are to each other as their mutual prayers ascend like the beautiful music of a harmonious symphony.

Moses: Personification of Humility

"And the man Moses was exceedingly humble – more than
any person on the face of the earth." (Numbers 12:3)

There are many aspects to the unique and towering personality of Moses which are clearly revealed in the Torah. This essay highlights a character trait which defined Moses throughout his life. While he exhibited powerful responses to injustices and carried out God's instructions without wavering, his self-deprecation was nothing short of amazing. One can only wonder how a man who was so unpretentious and modest could have achieved the great accomplishments that were his legacy. Perhaps, upon reflection, those character traits were the very cause for his greatness.

The reticence of Moses to assume any form of governance began with God's call to him to become the leader of his people. We go back to the Burning Bush which attracted his attention because it was in flames but would not be consumed. As Moses contemplated this phenomenon, he heard the voice of God commanding him to lead the Hebrew slaves out of Egypt. At this point, we read an extended dialogue between God and Moses in which he received many assurances that his mission would succeed. Moses, however, responded to each request with a reason why he was not up to such a challenge. Finally, when all other excuses failed, Moses concluded with the sharp response.

And he (Moses) said, "I beg you, my God, please send whomever you will send" (Exodus 4:13).

This response displeased God and the Torah tells us that, "The anger of God burned against Moses." It was at this point that a subtle element of a possible punishment crept into the dialogue. Whenever God is displeased, this displeasure is inevitably followed by some form of chastisement. Perhaps in this case it was God's offering to make Aaron, his brother, the primary representative to Pharaoh. Now we have ample precedents of the jealousy of brothers in the Torah. It began with Cain who was envious of Abel. We read of the struggles between Jacob and Esau, as well as the conflicts between Joseph and his brothers.

These were serious contentions and they all exhibited the surge of sibling rivalry that can cause severe damage to family relationships. Yet, Moses had no problem at all with his brother being cast into the light of prominence and was overjoyed to be reunited with him. What might have begun as a possible punishment of Moses did not turn out that way at all.

This sibling rivalry, however, is directed against Moses in another instance. We are informed that Miriam and Aaron, his sister and brother, spoke against him regarding the Ethiopian woman whom he had married. But they expanded their criticism by what seems to be rank jealousy.

"Did God speak only to Moses? Did God not speak to us as well?" (Numbers 12:1)

One can just imagine what kind of controversies this behavior could have generated in most families. Yet, after God severely castigated Miriam and Aaron, leaving Miriam with leprosy, Moses prayed for her recovery and, after a short period, she was healed. Despite this attack upon his personal life, Moses remained constant in his equanimity and exhibited no anger whatsoever.

A similar incident transpired concerning the leadership of Moses. On many occasions, the Torah describes how the people made demands upon Moses and stridently voiced their complaints and frustrations. In this case, they demanded meat and bemoaned their present restricted food availability as compared to a better diet in Egypt.

The pressure on Moses was so heavy and relentless that he begged God for help because he could not cope with the multitudes by himself. God told him to gather seventy elders to assist him in ruling the people. For a short period, these elders prophesied and then stopped. However, there were two elders - Eldad and Medad - who continued to prophesy. When it was reported to Joshua, he rushed to Moses and asked that these two be imprisoned for their subordination.

Imagine such a scene in a modern synagogue. Two unauthorized men take over the rabbi's pulpit and preach, as well as carry out sundry rabbinical duties. Not only would the congregation be in an uproar, but the rabbi would reasonably be expected to be quite upset himself.

Now read how Moses responded to Joshua:

> Are you jealous for my sake? Would that all God's people were prophets and God would put His spirit upon them. (Numbers 11:29)

There is a very poignant moment in the life of Moses prior to his death which again demonstrates his humility and total dedication to the will of God. As is well-known, Moses had two sons – Gershom and Eliezer. It can be assumed from a number of implied sources, that he wanted them to continue his leadership.

But it was not to be. God's plan was otherwise.

> And God said to Moses, take Joshua, the son of Nun, a man in whom is the (divine) spirit, and lay your **hand** upon him. (Numbers 27:18)

This act was to be a public indication that Moses, acting upon the will of God, was conferring the leadership of the people upon his successor.

Not only did Moses not attempt to dissuade God from this decision, but note the subtle change that Moses made in the act.

> And Joshua, the son of Nun, was full of the spirit of wisdom, for Moses had laid his **hands** upon him. (Deuteronomy 32:9)

Small wonder that he was the greatest prophet and leader to ever have lived. There are so many traits that we should attempt to emulate.

Women in the Exodus

The place of women in Jewish society has been a source of discussion and debate from time immemorial. As can be expected, there are those who vociferously claim that the status of women is far from what it should be, while others staunchly defend the position of the Jewish woman which is greatly superior to that of other cultures and are perfectly satisfied with the status quo.

There is no question that there are certain elements in the total body of Judaism in which the woman is burdened with problems that call for correction. One such example is the *Aguna*, a woman who cannot be released from an unhappy marriage because her husband refuses to give her a *Get* (Jewish divorce). Efforts are being made to bring this difficult matter to a successful conclusion. Nonetheless, it is without question that the totality of the situation ranks the Jewish woman head and shoulders above women in other cultures, including many contemporary societies. I believe that the small number of exceptions can and will be remedied in an orderly and halachic manner.

Men and women are not identical nor should they be. Each is unique and each supplements what the other lacks. Together they form a virtually divine unity.

If anyone feels that women are even slightly disregarded in Jewish tradition, I refer them to the Torah's account of the Exodus of the Israelites from their Egyptian bondage. I would like to review this climactic event with emphasis on the role of the women.

The first reference is found in the Talmudic Tractate of *Sotah* (12b), where we are introduced to the suffering of the Israelites under their

Egyptian servitude. The Talmud identifies Amram, a leader of his people, as divorcing his wife, Yocheved, because Pharaoh had decreed that all Jewish males were to be thrown into the Nile River. He commanded all the people to do the same. Miriam, his young daughter, challenged her father. She accused him of being harsher than the king of Egypt.

"Pharaoh's decree was only directed at the boys. Your plan will prevent the birth of both boys and girls," she argued.

So powerful was Miriam's protest that her parents were reunited and the Jewish slaves continued to procreate. The Torah then takes up the tale of two Jewish women who heroically protected and saved their people.

Shifra and Puah were two midwives. Pharaoh's orders to them were clear; they were to save the Jewish girls and drown the Jewish boys in the river. Both women bravely defied these cruel orders and refused to comply. When Pharaoh accused them of failing to abide by his commands, they responded that the Jewish women delivered their babies so quickly that they had no chance to obey.

So we already see how three women set the stage for the very survival of the Jewish slaves who were faced with annihilation by the Egyptians. Infant boys were still being murdered when Moses was born to Amram and Yocheved. The parents could not bring themselves to see their beloved son drowned, so they placed him into a little basket floating along the Nile.

Again, women came to the rescue. Bitya, the daughter of Pharaoh, was one of the righteous gentiles. When she came to the Nile to bathe, she saw the floating basket containing the beautiful baby and understood that it was a Jewish child. Instead of ordering to have him killed, she brought the basket to shore and decided to adopt the infant. She kept this a secret in defiance of her father.

But the story does not end here. Moses' sister, Miriam, again plays an active role. She carefully watched the progress of the basket containing her little brother. When she saw that the princess of Egypt had taken the baby and seemed to care for him, she approached her and offered to find a nursemaid.

Perhaps this is where the most amazing part of the story comes into play. The caretaker for the baby recommended by Miriam was none other than Yocheved, the mother of Moses! What a picture it must have been. Just one woman teaching her child what it means to be Jewish. As the baby grew, she explained to her son that he is not an Egyptian prince steeped in idol worship and persecution of others. She taught him that he is a descendant of Abraham, Isaac and Jacob and their great wives, Sarah, Rivka, Rachel and Leah. So powerful were the instructions of this single woman that Moses progressed to become the greatest prophet of the Jewish people!

But there is one more chapter in this saga.

Moses had to flee Egypt to Midian when it was discovered that he had killed an Egyptian who was mercilessly beating a slave. On his journey back to Egypt, he was accompanied by his wife, Tzipora, their son, Gershom and their newly born son, Eliezer. This infant had not yet been circumcised and it seems that Moses procrastinated in some manner in performing his *brit* (circumcision). The Torah informs us that God sought to kill him. Tzipora realized what was happening and immediately took a tool and circumcised Eliezer, thereby saving the life of Moses.

One wonders what would have happened to the enslaved Jewish community of Egypt if it were not for the bravery and dedication of its women from beginning to end. We are told that it was by the merit of the righteous women that we were redeemed from Egypt.

Of course, this is only one chapter. There are many other narratives of events before and after Egypt right up to the present time. One merely has to open the pages of the Bible or history books to learn of the vast contributions of Jewish women throughout the years. In a beautiful and quiet manner, they are the vanguard and backbone of our people.

Three Days of Darkness

The ninth of the Ten Plagues that were visited upon Egypt for their refusal to allow the Jewish slaves to leave their country is that of darkness. This plague, we are informed by the Torah, lasted for three days, during which the Egyptians could see nothing, but "for the Children of Israel there was light in their dwellings."

Since our Hebrew school days, we have had the image of a pitch black Egypt wherein, somehow, the Jews had light and were able to see everything.

This popular vision was questioned by the *Torah Temimah* (Rabbi Baruch Epstein 1886-1941). How could there be an uninterrupted period of three days of darkness? he asked, referring to a promise made by God after the Flood.

"Continuously, all the days of the earth, seedtime and harvest, cold and heat, summer and winter, **day and night**, shall not cease" (Genesis 8:22).

We know that, based upon God's promise, we can calculate the length of each day and night by a split second. How, then, could there be three consecutive nights without day?

I can add a question of my own. If an Egyptian and a Jew were standing next to each other, how would it be physically possible for one to be enmeshed in darkness, while the other was standing in bright light?

The answer of the *Torah Temimah* is simple, clear and brilliant. The days and nights did not alter their regular schedules. They remained the same as usual. However, the reason there was darkness for the Egyptians and they could not see is because God caused a cataract *(matbeya)* to be placed into their eyes, just as there were boils, etc. on their skin in other plagues. The Jews, on the other hand, did not suffer from this blemish in their eyes and for them there was light and they could see.

This ingenious explanation answers all questions and gives a sense of reality to the entire matter.

The lesson for us is that there are times when we allow ourselves to be blinded to situations which we should and could see more clearly. It is always necessary to strive for 20-20 spiritual eyesight.

When Did Moses Break the Tablets?

W hen Moses learned that the Children of Israel had begun to worship a Golden Calf in his forty day absence on Mount Sinai, it is well-known that he smashed the tablets on which the Ten Commandments were engraved. However, what is not as well-known is at exactly which point Moses committed this dramatic act. A close examination of this episode may be surprising in illuminating the matter.

We must immediately disabuse ourselves of the fallacious notion that Moses flew into a rage and shattered the Tablets as soon as he learned of the people's infamous deed. That is not at all the way the Torah describes it. Rather, Moses learned of their rebellious activities while he was still on Mount Sinai.

> And God spoke to Moses: "Go, get down, for your people ... have become corrupt. They have made themselves a molten calf, prostrated themselves to it and sacrificed to it." (Exodus 32: 7, 8)

Instead of exhibiting anger and even breaking the Tablets at that moment, Moses immediately began to plead on behalf of the people. It was only when God assured him that He would not destroy Israel for this rebellion that he began his descent and met Joshua at the bottom of the mountain. There was still no indication of Moses displaying anger or any other emotion until he came into full view of the congregation. That is when matters drastically changed.

> And it was when he drew near the camp and saw the calf **and the dances** that Moses' anger flared up. He threw down the Tablets from his hands and shattered them at the foot of the mountain. (Exodus 32:19)

This delayed reaction of Moses does not seem to conform to human nature. One would expect an explosive response upon hearing such upsetting news. Yet, from the time that God told Moses what had occurred until he saw what was taking place, we are not informed of even the slightest anger or rage.

I believe the key word to explain this is *u'mecholot* (and the dancing). This activity was not previously related to Moses. All he knew was that the people had fashioned a calf out of gold and were acting in a worshipful way toward it. It would be reasonable to assume that Moses took into account that the people had observed the idol worship of Egypt in their 210 years of servitude and were frightened when they thought their leader had become lost. They were desperate for leadership and Moses reasoned that he would point out the error they had committed and all would be well again.

It was only when Moses saw that they were joyfully dancing around the idol that rage overtook him, culminating in his smashing the Tablets as an everlasting lesson.

A more modern analogy may be drawn from a soldier who was inducted into the army during World War II. This was before many kosher arrangements had been made for the Jewish military and the soldier asked his rabbi what to do. The rabbi responded, "Eat what you must to survive and stay healthy, but don't lick your fingers."

Had they constructed the calf out of fear for their survival, things may have been very different. But their dancing demonstrated that they had turned their desperation into joyful activity. Therein lay the essence of their sin.

There is a great lesson in this for us all.

The Donkey That Spoke

N o, it is not a children's fairy tale. In fact, this event is clearly described in the Torah's Book of Numbers (Chapter 22).

The Children of Israel had wandered in the desert for a period of forty years and were heading toward Canaan. Challenged by the military might of nations along the way, they were victorious against all their enemies as they approached the Promised Land.

Balak, the king of Moab, was very concerned. Since he saw no way to achieve a military victory, he engaged the services of a heathen prophet named Balaam and asked him to curse the Jews. He felt that such a curse by a man who was considered a prophet among the nations, would have the effect of weakening or destroying the Jewish people.

Now Balaam belonged to that wretched group which re-surfaces again and again in history, whose *raison d'etre* is hatred of Jews. This fixation made him eager to undertake the mission which, as an added bonus, came with a huge reward. But no matter how hard he tried, the outcome was not as planned. Through divine intervention, the desired curses would not leave his mouth. Finally, at Balak's urging, he attempted a curse one last time and, in fact, blessed the Jewish people!

I'd like to focus on one part of the story which truly defies all logic, yet teaches a great deal. The section to which I refer is very mystical and extremely difficult to comprehend. As Balaam was riding on his donkey, a menacing angel blocked his way. The donkey sensed the presence of the angel and avoided it three times. Balaam, on the other hand, was totally unaware of the danger and was very angry that the donkey had stopped three times and veered off the path. He beat the hapless animal no less than three times.

Now comes the wonder of wonders. The Torah states that God opened the mouth of the donkey and the animal actually began to talk! He asked Balaam why he had beaten him three times and the prophet furiously responded that if he had had a sword, he would have killed the donkey. It was at this point that Balaam's eyes were opened in a way that allowed him to see the threatening angel. Suddenly Balaam realized that he had been terribly wrong and that it was a lowly donkey that had explained his error to him!

Maimonides, the great rationalist, explains this episode as having occurred in a dream or a vision. It would have been very difficult to assert that a donkey had acquired the gift of speech and the ability to inform his master of what was transpiring.

Maimonides' approach is similar in the story of Jacob wrestling with an angel as described in the book of Genesis. There, too, Maimonides maintains that Jacob experienced the entire scenario in a dream. Those who disagree ask how Jacob could have left the scene limping if it was only a dream. But the answer, especially in light of modern psychology, is clear. There can be psychosomatic effects which would actually translate into physical symptoms.

Others consider this matter to be perfectly acceptable within the confines of a miracle. According to both interpretations, however, one can ask the question as to what point is being made by the donkey speaking.

I would like to suggest that the Torah is teaching us that those who are obsessed with hatred of the Jewish people exist on such a low level that even a donkey could demonstrate to them how misguided they are. Balaam, who was driven by ill-will against the Children of Israel, was so blinded by his hatred that even his lowly beast of burden was in a position to lecture him.

This incident speaks to the many people who are so crazed by their prejudices and hatred that they lose their grip on reality and descend to depths lower than beasts.

There is one interesting addendum to this story. When Balaam attempted his last curse of the Children of Israel, the words that left his mouth were actually a blessing.

"How goodly are your tents, O Jacob, your dwelling places, O Israel" (Numbers 24:5).

This verse is recited until this day upon entering the synagogue. It has always seemed incomprehensible to me that we should give prominence to this evil prophet by quoting him each time we enter the synagogue. Do we not have enough beautiful verses from the book of Psalms and other sources that we must resort to a blessing which was rendered by someone who actually wanted to curse us?

There is no question in my mind that the Sages had a deeper meaning when they instructed us to recite this verse on a continual basis. On the one hand, it demonstrates the failure of our enemies. We survive and even thrive after their attempts to destroy us. We utilize their very words to show that their evil intentions have ended in dismal failure.

But there could well be another reason which has prophetic implications. We have endured the hatred and curses of many nations symbolized by Balaam. But we have the faith that the day will come when nations will surrender their hatred in exchange for brotherly love, which will then also be extended to the Jewish people. Thus we quote someone who much preferred to curse us than to bless us, in the knowledge and faith that those very words will one day turn into sincere love and respect.

"I Awaken the Dawn"
(Psalms 108:2)

There must be a deeper meaning to this statement by King David. After all, we know that night and dawn appear at precise times. Even a second has to be divided to calculate the exact moment. Was David implying that he had the power to determine the appearance of the dawn? Certainly not.

The natural daily appearance of the breaking of day has remained immutable for as long as history has been recorded and probably long before that. No effort by man has ever been able to change this daily natural occurrence by even a split second.

King David was clearly referring to a conceptual dawn within his emotional and spiritual frame of reference. The level of his lofty inspiration is reflected in the Book of Psalms written at different periods of his life. Even as a young man, he played the harp and the beautiful music which emanated from it soothed the psychological depressions of King Saul.

Strange as it seems, he was both a warrior and a poet who brilliantly excelled in both. His psalms are read by millions from generation to generation. His brave victory against Goliath is celebrated to this day.

So how did he awaken the dawn?

Blessed with great spirit, the onset of his inspiration was his personal dawn, regardless of the time. Whenever he was infused with this stirring and inspirational surge, it served as an inner and personal dawn which raised him to ever greater spiritual heights.

I believe that we are all able to be recipients of such elevating sparks, although the intensity may well be less than that of King David. It will depend on our individual nature and potential. But no matter. We can all rise to higher levels and instead of passively waiting for our dawn, we should actively summon it and thereby greatly illuminate our lives.

We Are All Job

T he message of the book of Job (*Iyov*) is so difficult to comprehend that one almost feels that the attempt is an exercise in futility. The book endeavors to explain – even to justify – the tribulations which come upon innocent individuals.

Job is described as a good man who exhibits all the virtues of a pious and decent human being. He is God-fearing and "whole and straightforward." His home life is serene and blessed. He has an attentive wife, seven sons and three daughters. He is more prosperous than all of his neighbors and is the owner of huge flocks that greatly enrich him. Job sponsors many banquets to which all his friends are invited. After each such banquet, Job would offer expiation sacrifices in the event that any of his children may have acted inappropriately.

The book takes us from this wonderful scenario of a happy and successful family to the mystical heights of heaven. There, on a certain day, which the commentaries identify as Rosh Hashana, God praises Job to Satan, describing him as an example of the just and upright.

Satan, the perennial Accuser, insidiously responds that Job is not religious in vain. He has been rewarded for his piety with a wonderful family and huge riches. Small wonder, mocks Satan, that he is pious!

At this point, the trial of Job began. It is interesting and crucial to note that Satan could not take any action on his own, but needed permission from God to bring any misfortune upon Job. The book clearly demonstrates that God reigns supreme and that there are no independent powers beside Him.

And so, Satan received permission to divest Job of all his riches, although at this point he was not permitted to cause any harm to Job's body. Reports soon came to Job of disaster after disaster. All his flocks died, his buildings were in ruin and his ten children died in one of his houses which had collapsed.

Despite his agony and grief, Job remained steadfast. He rent his clothing, fell upon the ground and uttered the famous words, "The Lord has given and the Lord has taken, blessed be the name of the Lord."

But Job's misery was to go a step further. Satan countered God's praise of Job's faithfulness by claiming that as long as his body was not touched, he was able to maintain his belief. At this point God permitted Satan to strike Job's body, but not to endanger his life. The result was that his skin became inflamed with boils from head to toe.

With this background, the book goes into circuitous discussions between Job and his friends, most of whom attempted to justify Job's disasters as a result of his sins. Job staunchly denies that he has sinned and asks God to vindicate him to his friends by admitting that his misery was not the result of punishment for any sins that he may have committed.

Finally, after many chapters, God answers Job with an implied rebuke both to him and his friends for attempting to understand His mysterious ways. Job is told that he was not present at the creation of the world, nor can he begin to understand the intrinsic forces and movements which are the lifeline of the universe. Upon being confronted with this awesome declaration by God, Job humbly admits that his knowledge is infinitesimal and that it was wrong of him to question God, even under the dire circumstances in which he found himself. His three friends are rebuked for their attempts to wrongly justify God's actions and Job is asked to pray for them.

It is at this point that Job's tribulations cease. His prosperity is returned to him in far greater proportion than what he had lost. It is interesting to note that he again became the father of seven sons and three daughters, the same number as before the disasters that had befallen him. Job lived many years after his tribulations and saw four more generations in his lifetime.

So the saga of Job ends on a positive note. Despite all his agony, he was blessed with a measure of divine explanation and a restoration to his former state. I am left, however, with a very troubling question and problem. What about his original seven sons and three daughters? They were killed when his house collapsed. How are we to come to terms with their fate?

The only possible solution that I can accept is that each and every one of us reflects Job. We are all born and die and experience a lifetime of events. None of us has been given the reasons for any of these occurrences. The only answer which can help us navigate through our daily experiences is God's answer to Job. Where knowledge and wisdom cease, faith must replace them.

When all is said and done, everyone is Job.

A Share For All

"All Israel has a share in *Olam Haba* (the World
to Come)." *(*Tractate Sanhedrin 90:)

This is the opening verse of the introductory Mishna to each of the six
chapters of *Pirkei Avot* (Ethics of the Fathers). These words seem to
be problematic. Is the Mishna actually stating that by the very act of one's
birth into the Jewish faith, a guarantee is automatically extended to achieve
Olam Haba, regardless of what type of life the person lived? There are those
who make this very case. They claim that there is a mystical quality of
sanctity attached to every Jewish soul which in and of itself qualifies the
person for a place in *Olam Haba*.

Yet, the Talmud in Sanhedrin immediately following this Mishna
apparently disagrees. A long list is presented which excludes those who are
in violation from being able to enter *Olam Haba*, because of their serious
deviations from the required Torah way of life.

The apparent contrast between the Mishna and the Talmud raises
a most serious problem. The word *kol* (all), is clearly all-inclusive. It is
utilized to indicate that each and every Jew has an actual share in *Olam
Haba*. How can the Talmud then list exclusions - and quite of few of
them – thereby creating what appears to be a direct contradiction of the
Mishna?

Upon reflection, I believe that there is actually no conflict between
the Mishna and the Talmud. Once we delve deeper and understand the
Mishna's message, the teaching of the Talmud which follows is a natural
extension.

Let us assume a person is waiting for ten guests. He likes them very much and prepares a delicious cake for them. According to the number of guests expected, he cuts the cake into ten slices and places it upon the table. The guests arrive and take their seats. Each guest is presented with a piece of the cake. It is each one's choice whether to accept or reject what has been offered. Regardless of what action they take, a slice of the cake has been reserved for each of them. In other words, each was given the opportunity to take and enjoy the prepared share.

Herein lies the message of the Mishna. God, in His love for His people, has prepared the Torah which is freely presented to each and every Jew. Whether or not it will be accepted is a personal and individual decision based upon the free choice which every human being has been granted. The Torah is the gateway to *Olam Haba*. Thus, each and every Jew to whom the Torah has been offered clearly has access to the path which will lead him /her to this desired goal. If that way of life will be rejected or certain behaviors will be practiced which are diametrically opposed to the teachings of the Torah, the share which was inherently offered, will be rejected and withdrawn.

The Mishna states that a share is available for the taking and that this share can be achieved through making the effort of following the teachings of the Torah. The ensuing Talmud defines actions which will cancel this share, but it certainly does not negate the premise of "All Israel" - that each and every Jew has the *potential* to receive a share in *Olam Haba*.

Do as I Say

When all is said and done, it must be realized that the great sages of the Talmud were human beings with character flaws and strengths like all of us. I specifically refer to Hillel and Shammai, whose teachings and fame extended throughout the generations.

Hillel was known for his unending patience and serenity in all his dealings with others. Most reflective of this characteristic is the Talmudic account in Tractate *Shabbat* (31a) about the man who made a wager that he could cause Hillel to lose his temper. To bring this about, he continued to knock on Hillel's door on the eve of Shabbat, when he knew that Hillel was bathing in preparation for the forthcoming Sabbath. Time and again, Hillel came to the door, in a bathrobe and dripping, to patiently answer the frivolous questions which the man posed. He desperately tried to arouse the sage's ire, but to no avail. To his chagrin, Hillel responded each time with patience and a reasonable reply, despite the silliness of the queries. Finally, it was the man who became angry and said, "I lost four hundred 'zuz,' because you did not lose your patience." To which Hillel responded, "My son, better you should lose four hundred 'zuz' many times than I should lose my patience."

On the other side of the coin, Shammai was very short-tempered. He did not have nearly the amount of patience as his contemporary, Hillel. On the same page of the Talmud, it is related that a gentile came to Shammai and asked to be converted to the Jewish religion while he stood on one leg. With a stick in his hand, Shammai chased him from the room.

When the man appeared before Hillel with the same request, Hillel said, "What is hateful to you, do not do unto your neighbor. The rest of the teachings are merely commentary."

All of the above raises a question regarding a famous statement by Shammai in Tractate *Avot*, "and receive all men with a pleasing disposition" (1:15).

How can this be? This statement obviously belies the actions of this great sage as described in the Talmud!

The answer is subtle, but very compelling. Shammai may not always have been proud of or satisfied with his angry responses. Perhaps he would have preferred to be as gentle as Hillel, but his nature did not always permit it. An analogy may be drawn from a drunkard who strongly advises everyone to abstain from excessive liquor. He is not a hypocrite. On the contrary. He is in a better situation than others to warn of the dangers of alcoholism.

And so it was with the great sage, Shammai. He certainly loved and respected his fellow human beings. Yet, there were times when he was given to moments of anger. In the full knowledge that this was not ideal behavior, he advised one and all to greet people in a friendly manner and endeavor to be patient with them.

Rabbi Meir and Women

R abbi Meir was one of the greatest third generation *Tanna'im* who lived in the time of the Mishna. It is of great interest that among his voluminous teachings, he authored an extremely controversial blessing which has been part of the morning service throughout the generations. The blessing is recited daily by men and expresses gratitude to God that, "He has not made me a woman." Although many reasons have been forwarded with a view of making this blessing more palatable, the fact remains that its construction is quite negative and could be construed to project women in an inferior position.

Rabbi Baruch Epstein (1860-1942) comments on this blessing as follows: "Rabbi Meir formulated this daily blessing based upon a section in the Talmudic tractate *Menachot* (43b) which characterized women in a manner that rendered them low in his eyes due to their simple-mindedness" (*Torah Temima* 24a).

There is further evidence regarding Rabbi Meir's opinion of women in the tractate of *Bava Batra* (16b): "And God blessed Abraham *bakol* (with everything). Rabbi Meir states: '(The blessing) *with everything* indicates that Abraham did not have a daughter.'"

From the above, one might arrive at the conclusion that Rabbi Meir had somewhat of a negative opinion of women. If so, it would be interesting if a possible cause for this attitude could be determined. Based purely on conjecture, it is noteworthy that his wife was the famous Beruriah, who was renowned for her vast wisdom. She was involved in contemporary Talmudic decisions and greatly praised for her knowledge. In the tractate of *Pesachim* (62b), it is stated that she learned three-hundred *halachot* (laws) from three-hundred teachers in one day. Now while this is obviously presented with more than a touch of hyperbole, it is quite clear that her acumen was on the highest level.

She could also be quite sharp. The Tractate *Eruvin* (53b) relates that once Rabbi Yose asked her, "Which is the direction to Lod?" She sharply criticized him for framing the question to her in this manner. A man conversing with a woman should greatly curtail his words. According to her, he should simply have asked, "Where to Lod?"

The Midrash on Psalms (Chapter 118), tells how Rabbi Meir was greatly disturbed by the noise some of his neighbors were making. In a moment of anger, he exclaimed, "May these sinners die." She corrected him by saying that he should pray for the abolition of sin, not the sinners.

One cannot help but wonder if some form of frustration may not have impelled Rabbi Meir to formulate such a blessing and author other less than flattering comments about women. None of these observations should be misconstrued to detract from the greatness of Rabbi Meir or to suggest any unwarranted bias on his part. My purpose is purely to try to analyze the sayings and opinions of some of our great scholars in the total context of their experiences.

What Will My Neighbors Say?

I quote the following from the Talmud because of an incident which I observed when I was a rabbinical student. The incident itself was quite commonplace, but it somehow had implications that have always remained with me.

> When Rabbi Yochanan ben Zakkai fell ill, his disciples came to visit him and said to him, "Our master, bless us." He replied, "May it be God's will that the fear of heaven shall be as great upon you as the fear of mortal man." His disciples asked, "Is that all?" He replied," Would that you might attain even that much fear!" (*Berachot* 28b)

There was a Hebrew bookstore right across the street from Yeshiva University where I studied. I would spend quite a bit of time there wishing I had the money to buy all the available books, but simply perusing them with a view to someday making them my property. On one such day, a man burst into the store asking if they sold *mezuzot*. Of course he received an affirmative reply. Could there be a Jewish bookstore where *mezuzot* were not available?

"I am so relieved," sighed the gentleman. "You see, I have been living in an apartment building for quite a few weeks and I have not yet affixed a *mezuza* on my door. "What will my neighbors think?"

What, indeed?

Seize the Moment

A deeply instructive anecdote is related in the Babylonian Talmud in Tractate *Berachot* (27:-28.) concerning the proposed appointment of Rabbi Elazar ben Azariah to the position of head of the Sanhedrin (Supreme Court). When he discussed this matter with his wife, she expressed some doubt.

"Perhaps they will depose you," she said.

He replied with an analogy.

"There is a maxim," he replied. "Use your precious bowl on the day that you have it, even if it may be broken tomorrow."

He pointed out that it is a mistake to be overly cautious about the future. As long as reasonable considerations and precautions are taken, one should accept what is offered and continue on. In other words, it is prudent to proceed with caution, but not with fear. I believe that this is sage advice for all.

JEWISH HISTORY AND THE LAND OF ISRAEL

"My claim to being Jewish is not because my parents are Jewish - it is because my grandchildren are Jewish."
(Rabbi Norbert Weinberg)

Genesis of Anti-Semitism

The roots of anti-Semitism extend to the remotest antiquity. The accepted genesis of this scourge of civilization is thought to be the enslavement of the Israelites by ancient Egypt. However, a closer reading of the Torah will show that it dates to a much earlier period.

In Genesis (14:13), Abraham, (then still called Abram), is informed that his nephew, Lot, had been kidnapped by a conglomeration of four kings. This is the first time that he is described as *ha'Ivri*, the Hebrew. Perhaps we are so informed because the reason for his being kidnapped was because he was a Hebrew, which would mark this as the first anti-Jewish act. In an Entebbe type of forceful response, Abraham gathered an army of 318 soldiers, pursued the kidnappers all the way to the northern territory of Dan, and rescued Lot.

Later, there was a great deal of trouble and strife regarding the wells which Abraham had dug and which the Philistines had blocked. This continued into the next generation, when the Torah informs us that, "Isaac had become great and kept becoming greater until he was very great…and the Philistines envied him" (Genesis 26:13). The result of this envy was that Abimelech ordered Isaac to leave because, "You have become mightier than us." It was at that point that Isaac undug all the wells of his father, which had been jammed by the Philistines after Abraham's death. How many times in history has this chapter been repeated almost to the minutest detail?

The strained relationship between Jacob and Esau was certainly a harbinger of the future, especially in light of the fact that Esau was the progenitor of Rome and of ensuing Christianity.

The final episode upon which I want to focus regarding this subject is the treatment which Laban accorded to his son-in-law, Jacob. After suffering and overcoming Laban's treachery and deceit for no less than twenty years, Jacob became a wealthy man. He worked hard and remained loyal to all the agreements he had made with Laban. His wealth was obtained by honest labor but, as happened with his father and countless future Jewish generations, Laban's sons became jealous and hated him. Jacob took his wives and family and prepared to leave his father-in-law's home.

Laban pursued him and asked why he had left surreptitiously, thereby preventing a farewell celebration. Apparently, by this time, Jacob had had enough and vehemently rebuked Laban for the way he had been treated.

It was at this point that Laban responded exactly the way future anti-Semites have acted toward the Jewish people.

"The daughters are my daughters, the children are my children and the flock is my flock, and all that you see is mine" (Genesis 31:43).

How many times in history have the Jewish people worked diligently in a country in which they were loyal and productive citizens only to become the source of jealousy and hatred by the majority population? How many times, after passing unlawful legislation, has all Jewish property been expropriated to the persecuting government which considered Jewish possessions to be their own?

The above, which only scratches the surface, should bear clear testimony that the Egyptian exile was far from the beginning. Even at the time of Joseph, who saved Egypt from the disaster of the great famine, Hebrews lived in great opulence in Egypt. When Joseph arranged a meal to celebrate his reunion with his brothers, the Torah tells us, "They served him (Joseph) separately ... and the Egyptians who ate with him separately, for the Egyptians could not bear to eat food with the Hebrews, it being loathsome to Egyptians" (Genesis 43:30).

Although this was long before the Egyptian slavery began, the cycle of persecution had already begun. Jews, as a minority working hard and successfully, became productive citizens, only to arouse the hatred and jealousy of their neighbors. And so it continued for centuries to come.

The seeds and results of anti-Semitism are almost mystical since they defy logical explanation. The greatest ray of hope to the ultimate elimination of this curse upon mankind is the return of the Jewish people to their ancient homeland. It is there, and only there, that they belong and from there, the ultimate salvation will emanate for all mankind.

Those "Brave" Anti-Semites

"And I will bless those who bless you and curse
those who curse you" (Genesis 12:3).

These are the fateful words which accompanied Abraham, the first Hebrew, as he left his homeland and began his journey toward the unknown Promised Land. During that long span of time, the Jewish people have experienced every form of discrimination, hatred and subjugation which could possibly be contrived by distorted minds bent on evil. Utilizing all efforts to survive despite the tremendous odds against them, the Jewish people have not only overcome each period of persecution, but have emerged stronger and greater.

Throughout this time, the above verse from the Bible has been vindicated in an almost mystical manner. Many nations and empires have ruthlessly persecuted their Jewish minorities. Invariably, these nations have disintegrated and disappeared from the stage of history. The Jewish people, on the other hand, have not only survived, but have thrived and gained strength at each interval.

This essay does not profess to be an exhaustive historical analysis, but is merely an attempt to present a few examples. The first celebrated persecution of the Jewish people, then still known as Hebrews, was at the hands of biblical Egypt. Joseph had saved Egypt from seven punishing years of famine and Egypt's response was to enslave the Jews. Moreover, fearing the usurping of his throne by a Hebrew child, Pharaoh decreed that all male Jewish children be thrown into the Nile River. The rest of the story is well-known. Egypt suffered virtual destruction as a result of the Ten

Plagues and Pharaoh and his army drowned in the Red Sea. Thus, Pharaoh suffered the same fate that he had imposed upon the Jewish people. The Children of Israel, who had entered Egypt with Jacob as a small tribe, now left as a mighty and determined nation.

No less dramatic is the fate of Spain in 1492. Once again, Jewish culture and commerce helped raise Spain to become a leading world power. The Jewish contributions to Spain's culture, art and commerce contributed to that period which became known as the Golden Age of Spain. Spain's response was a vicious attack against its Jewish citizens by imposing the infamous Inquisition, which culminated in the expulsion of its Jewish population. Spain, which had hitherto been a leading luminary among the nations of the world, was now reduced to mediocrity, from which it never rose again. Once again, the above biblical prophecy was totally vindicated.

The unspeakable evil which was visited upon the world in general and upon the Jewish people in particular by Germany and the Nazis during World War II needs no further description. The utter evil of the Holocaust condemned it to a travesty virtually beyond human comprehension. Again, Germany's Jewish population had played a great part in the country's success. Jewish soldiers served in World War I, and besides famous personalities such as Albert Einstein and Sigmund Freud, the average citizen contributed greatly to Germany's prominence among the nations. The barbarity and savagery with which Germany turned upon its Jewish population and Jews everywhere, will remain a black page in history forever. After causing horrendous destruction and the annihilation of millions of innocent lives, its end followed a predictable path. Hitler was shot and cremated, and his country suffered destruction, humiliation and defeat. Although it was small comfort to the victims, it was on the heels of the Holocaust that the State of Israel was born. Once again, the ancient words of the Torah were vindicated and came true.

One other empire of sorts should be listed. For over seven decades, the Communist regime in Russia suppressed religion in general and Judaism in particular. Its leaders boasted that universal communism was inevitable and that it would rule the world. Forced to keep their faith surreptitiously, the Jewish community continued its traditions under virtually impossible circumstances. At rare times, they would dance publicly in front of synagogues on Jewish holidays and pay dearly for their courage. Suddenly, the entire communist system collapsed. Thousands of Russian Jews emigrated to Israel, becoming one of the major ethnic groups in the new Jewish state.

On the other side of the coin, the United States has consistently served as the hope of mankind. There are certainly areas which require improvement and serious problems that demand solutions. Nevertheless, the degree of freedom and lack of minority oppression far surpass that of most other countries in the world. For decades, America has remained the leading world power. Its Statue of Liberty continues to send its beacon of liberty to the homeless and oppressed.

Given the above examples, and there are numerous others, one wonders what gives the Jew-haters the actual courage to pursue their hateful agenda. Have they never heard of the Bible and the divine promises of blessing or curse which have never failed?

It is my contention that this brand of hatred, which the world chooses to label anti-Semitism, is a form of animosity which is actually a mental and emotional aberration, a disease which is extremely contagious. It must be remembered that this malady has been nurtured for over two millennia by the Church, whose theology and practice demonized the Jewish religion from its very beginning. It is not within the purview of this essay to analyze reasons for these hatreds, except to state that they made the deepest impressions upon millions of people throughout the generations whose prejudices and contempt for the Jewish religion was passed from generation to generation. It is only within the last few decades, beginning sometime after World War II, that popes have begun to disavow the past and make efforts to erase these animosities from their theology and their people.

But the roots of anti-Semitism are not only in Christianity; they find expression where blame for poverty or other communal ills are somehow placed on the Jewish minority. In all cases, there is no relation between the reality of the situation and the calumny thrust upon Judaism. Throughout history, Jewish citizens have been productive and law-abiding. They have placed education as their highest priority and, wherever permissible, have made great contributions to the countries in which they lived. Perhaps being a successful minority among an unsuccessful majority produces a lethal combination.

I warn anyone considering a life of hating Jews and trying to harm them in any way to proceed with the greatest caution. Even a cursory knowledge of the Bible, as well as historical reactions to the hatred of Jews, should cause such a person to think twice before embarking on such a course which seems to inevitably end in failure.

I conclude by stating my belief that the hatred of Jews is a malady totally devoid of logic. Its powers of infection and contagion can be disastrous. It is to be hoped that as this madness loses its appeal, anti-Semitism will become an anachronism as civilization moves into a better and healthier state.

Encourage the Arab Boycott

One of the battlefields utilized by the Arab anti-Israeli machinery is the boycott of all Israeli products. Companies which trade with Israel in any form are blacklisted. As in many other situations, people and countries have shown their true character in this area. Many have succumbed in order to gain a degree of commercial advantage. They are prepared to sell their souls for a bit of profit. A vast majority of others, on the other hand, would have none of it. They continue an open market with Israel. If, as a result, the Arabs decide to blacklist them, so be it.

I have a somewhat novel idea on this matter. I believe that if the Arabs insist on pursuing this repugnant course, they should do it in a logical and thorough manner. They should be openly consistent in their blind and phobic hatred and carry the boycott to its ultimate conclusion, regardless of the consequences.

Let me start by suggesting that they sever all connections with Abraham, whom the Torah names as the first Hebrew. But I believe that they have already dealt with that matter by claiming that Abraham was a Moslem, and so was Moses! Explaining to them that Abraham and Moses preceded the founder of the Muslim religion would merely be confusing the issue with the facts.

But getting a little closer to the present, it seems to me that in the interest of consistency, every Arab should refuse to shop in the beautiful Israeli malls, refrain from dining in restaurants and cafés, and certainly not utilize any Israeli hospital. As it presently stands, Arabs happily roam about all Israeli shopping centers, are quite visible in the abundance of restaurants and avail themselves of the finest medical services in the Middle East - and possibly the world.

It is a most interesting phenomenon to see how well and equally they are treated in all these and other areas when, at the same time, a Jewish person who might have gotten lost in an Arab town would be lucky to escape with his life. How long this imbalance will be tolerated is beyond me.

But that is only scratching the surface. There are so many more areas in which the Arabs can and should shore up their boycotting efforts.

A good place to start would be their complete refusal to take the anti-polio vaccine which was discovered by Jonas Salk who was clearly Jewish. The fact that this could cause huge epidemics of Infantile Paralysis among them could be used to good advantage. Of course they could blame it on the Jews. In fact, only a short while ago, one of their top spokesmen stated that the Talmud encourages drug traffic. This type of blame also has more than enough precedent. Jews were blamed for having caused the bubonic plague. The real reason why they suffered less than the general population from this disease is no doubt because they followed their religious dictates by scrupulously washing their hands before partaking of food.

Or they could follow the example of their mentor, Adolf Hitler, who blamed the Jews for every conceivable malady instead of focusing on the Germans who were unable to cope with their problems.

Of great interest is the fact that since 1901, no less than 197 Jewish people have been awarded the Nobel Prize, who have made huge contributions to the betterment of mankind. Of course, the Arabs who are bent upon the destruction of Israel, Judaism and Western civilization can console themselves by happily claiming responsibility for untold numbers of suicide bombings and similar acts of terror, causing death and destruction to civilian men, women and children. There is hardly a Nobel Prize recipient among their masses.

But back to the boycott which is so strenuously pursued by the Arab countries. Any loyal Arab should not permit himself to be tested for syphilis because the Wasserman test was developed by a Jew, August Paul Wasserman, who was also the president of the Academy for Knowledge of Judaism. Should the boycotter discover that he has contracted the disease, he should bear it with resignation because the antidote, Salvarsan, was developed by Paul Ehrlich - a Jew!

Diabetes is another great enemy to people's health, but a good Arab should refrain from seeking a cure via insulin because it was developed by Dr. Oskar Minkowski who, incidentally, had to flee from the anti-Semitism of the Tzar's government. Had he been left alone as a Jew contributing to the world's welfare, he might have been able to achieve even more benefits to mankind.

Digitalis, a potent antidote to heart disease, should never be used by a loyal Arab who wishes to abide by the anti-Israel boycott because Dr. Ludwig Traube had the temerity to offer this great blessing to humanity. In fact, he managed to produce all these benefits despite being persecuted for his Jewish ancestry in the 1870's in Berlin.

If an Arab should develop a headache from all this information, he must grin and bear it but, under no circumstances may he seek relief with Pyramidon, because of the involvement of another Jew - Karl Spiro.

The terrible disease of tuberculosis, which wrought havoc on society before the advent of Zalman Waxman - yes, another Jew - who invented the wonder drug of Streptomycin, must be shunned by all good Arabs as they bravely make the great sacrifice of falling victim to this horrible malady.

Now it is true that many have suspected the screeching and patently false accusations by Arab spokesmen as being the result of mental malfunctions ranging from delusions to phobic ranting. Should this be the case, one would think that they should avail themselves of psychoanalysis, which may restore them to a semblance of sanity. But alas, foiled again! Psychotherapy, as is generally known, was developed by the great mind of Sigmund Freud, who is listed in the annals of the Jewish people.

Perhaps it would be a good idea for the hate mongers in the Arab world to calm down and begin a positive program of elevating the dismal conditions of their fellow Arabs in the refugee camps and similar slums. Perhaps they might consider emulating the Israelis who emptied out their refugee camps after thousands of Jews were driven out of Arab countries and came to Israel. Within two years, all the inhabitants of these temporary camps were integrated into Israeli society and became productive citizens. But it seems that the petro-trillions of dollars amassed by the Arab rulers are not available for such beneficial purposes. Israel's budget was tight, but they succeeded in their goal. The Arabs, tragically, have cynically left their brothers and sisters to languish in the dismal conditions of squalid camps to be utilized for their nefarious propaganda purposes.

So I hope that the Arab leaders who espouse perennial hatred will study these Jewish products and undertake a systematic and complete boycott of them. I want to assure them that these are just random pickings - there are many, many more to choose from.

Perhaps - just perhaps – they may sustain a stroke of rational thought and come to the realization that they are on a course of self-destruction, as were all the Jew-haters before them. Armed with such a realization, and coupled with the knowledge of all the myriads of Jewish contributions upon which their very lives hang, they may decide to give up their madness and embark on a course which will benefit their masses and put them on a path which will bring peace and prosperity to themselves and the world.

Where is Babylonia?

There is extremely strong resistance in traditional Judaism regarding the removal of any restrictions that have developed in the course of time, even if the conditions that initially brought about these constraints may have become totally obsolete. This observation also applies to the text of our prayers. If we once prayed for a certain place or situation and the conditions which initiated those prayers have changed or disappeared, very few authorities will favor their deletion.

One of the defenses of this situation is that any prayers or customs that have been accepted by the Jewish people have become so enshrined that their elimination would be unthinkable.

A more practical explanation would be that at the present, we do not have the advantage of the Sanhedrin, the Jewish Supreme Court, which would have the authority to change or delete any current Jewish customs or introduce new ones. However, many customs and prohibitions continue to appear and become accepted without being formalized by any religious judicial body and simply commence with a life of their own.

I have another thought on the matter which seems to me to be very functional. All our customs and prohibitions, regardless of their origin, may be compared to bars around a cage in the zoo. If even some of these constraints are removed, the animals may rush out and disperse in every direction. This is known in halachic parlance as *poretz geder* (breaking the fence). The result is that there is an enduring reluctance to allow the discontinuation of any *minhag* (custom).

I am writing this essay a few days before the Fast of Tisha B'Av, the sad commemoration of the destruction of both Holy Temples in Jerusalem.

This brings to mind a short prayer which is inserted into the *Amida* on the afternoon of the Fast.

It petitions God to:

> Console the mourners of Zion and Jerusalem and the city
> which is in mourning, destroyed, disgraced and in ruins.
> It has no sons (residents) and no one living in it. Its head
> is bowed like a barren woman who did not bear children.

At face value, it would be impossible to reconcile these statements with the reality of Jerusalem today. The city is not in mourning, disgraced or in ruins. It has, thank God, so many residents that its traffic is usually snarled and its real estate demands are at an all-time high. Its head is not bowed like a barren woman, but it stands proud as a beacon of light not only to Israel, but to the Jewish people and the world.

The late chief rabbi of Israel, Rabbi Shlomo Goren (1917-1994), composed a revised version of this prayer wherein he tried to maintain its ancient meaning, yet bring it into the reality of the present. Although his version is presented in some prayer books next to the traditional form, the overwhelming majority of rabbis and *poskim* (decisors) strongly reject the new version and counsel the retention of the traditional one.

Far be it from me to question, certainly not quarrel with these *poskim*. My intention is to simply demonstrate the reluctance of any change in these matters, regardless of opposing evidence.

There are innumerable examples to point out the above, but there is one other illustration I would like to present. I refer to the prayer recited every Shabbat morning beginning with *Yekum Purkan* ("May deliverance arise"). In it, there is an Aramaic prayer for the students in the schools of Israel and Babylonia.

Again, the reality of the situation is clear. There is no Babylonia today! The country referred to is now Iraq. There are a few prayer books that have substituted or added words, such as "and all the countries of our dispersion." The vast majority of synagogues and prayer books, however, have maintained the original text for the "Jews of Babylonia," a country which has not been in existence for centuries!

Of course, we can always argue that God knows the real intention of our prayers, but we are generally counselled to be precise in our supplications. This is clearly indicated when Jacob made an appeal to God.

"And if He will give me bread to eat and clothes to wear" (Genesis 28:20).

At first glance, it seems quite redundant of Jacob to ask for bread to eat. What else would he do with bread? Similarly, why request clothing to wear? Is that not the purpose of clothing?

But Jacob wanted to be extremely precise in his petitions. He did not want to own bread and be unable to eat and enjoy it. He wanted the appetite which good health affords to consume the bread. Similarly, Jacob did not simply ask to be in possession of clothing. Again, he wanted to be able to wear them in good health.

The Halacha actually follows Jacob's formula. It teaches that while we should stay within the parameters of our public prayers, we are to be very clear in our personal petitions.

Why, then, are we so inaccurate in our prayers by appealing to God for the non-existent Jews of Babylonia and the restoration of a destroyed Jerusalem bereft of its inhabitants?

My final example, although there are many others, is the matter of *kitniyot* or legumes. It is a known fact that *chametz* (leavened food), is strictly forbidden throughout the festival of Passover. In early medieval France and somewhat later, in Ashkenazi Rhineland, Germany, a number of food items, which resembled *chametz*, were used interchangeably year-round. Examples of these items are rice, corn, beans, peas, peanuts and lentils. Because of the fear that they may be mixed with the forbidden *chametz,* the Ashkenazic Jews of that area refrained from eating any of these legumes on Passover. The Sephardic Jews were not affected by this stricture and, to this day, eat *kitniyot* on the festival.

The point is that the conditions which caused the prohibitions at that time have become archaic and obsolete. Today, government regulations clearly define food products such as *chametz* foods and the above-mentioned legumes. No one claims that these legumes are actually *chametz.*

Yet, the ban on legumes has not been lifted in Ashkenazic communities. In Israel, there are restaurants which advertise their menus as including *kitniyot* and others which do not serve them.

It is hard to define the reason for this hesitation. Perhaps it is the inability or unwillingness of our religious leaders to make the effort of coming together to permit that which should clearly be allowed nowadays.

Although it is a serious matter, perhaps a light comment will conclude this analysis.

The question was asked as to how many Orthodox rabbis it would take to change a lightbulb. The immediate answer was an incredulous "*Change?*" Perhaps enough rabbis will join together soon to cast a much needed new light to bring these aspects of Halacha into contemporary reality.

The Unique Egg

E ach year we place a hard-boiled egg on our Seder plate. This egg represents the festival sacrifice which was offered on Passover along with the *Korban Pesach* (the Paschal lamb). Although any cooked food product would satisfy this requirement, the egg has invariably been the accepted choice.

There is good reason for this.

The basic purpose for cooking foods is to soften them. Raw meat or potatoes would not be welcome on our dinner table. Interestingly, there is one food item which defies this process and acts in direct opposition to the norm. The egg, in its natural state, is not only soft, it is liquid. As it continues to be boiled, it gets harder and harder until it turns into what is known as the hard-boiled egg.

Jewish tradition offers a great lesson regarding this process.

Historically, many nations and empires rose to a pinnacle and enjoyed a period of virtually uncontested power, after which they began to show a steady decline. The greater the military or political pressure which was brought upon them, the quicker they deteriorated and disappeared from the arena of history. This was the fate of ancient Egypt, the Greek and Roman empires, among many others.

In sharp contrast, the Jewish people never appeared in history as a world power. They lived peacefully and made huge contributions in every aspect of human endeavor, far beyond their number. Nevertheless, they were continually persecuted and set upon by much more powerful nations. These oppressions and persecutions would easily have made much stronger powers dissolve and disappear. However, the Jewish people not only repeatedly survived, but they invariably rose from their persecution to a higher and stronger level than their previous condition.

Perhaps even more amazing is the fact that when left undisturbed and well-treated, the tendency of Jewish communities has been to become careless in the observance of their traditions and lapse into assimilation.

This is the fascinating resemblance to the egg. Left in its natural state, it is liquid and can easily break. Only when the pressure of heat is applied does it become hard and firm.

I am writing this essay in Israel and was reminded of the egg metaphor only yesterday. A horrible terrorist attack was committed by an Arab who drove his truck into a group of soldiers, killing four young people and wounding a number of others. The civilized countries denounced this act, while the terrorist organizations and their adherents gleefully applauded and called the perpetrator a hero.

When this type of attack occurs, the entire Israeli community merges into a tightly knit family. Thousands attend the funerals and the bereaved families are the center of everyone's love and care. Under normal circumstances, Israelis have the tendency to argue and engage in endless debates. But their seemingly strident and aggressive differences are reasonably superficial, especially in the face of a common danger.

And herein lies the basic mistake that the enemies of Israel are making. The more they bluster and terrorize, the stronger and more united the people of Israel become. In many ways, it reverses the normal rules of society. The precedents of these responses are massive, going all the way back to the biblical enslavement of the Israelite slaves in Egypt. Logically, they should have been annihilated at that point in history. The pressure on those slaves was so severe that they should have vanished as a people then and there. Yet, their oppressors were totally defeated and they emigrated from the country as a free people. Egypt has never been a world power since that time.

The Greek and Roman empires ruthlessly oppressed the Jewish people, as did Spain during the Inquisition, as well as many others. They are now in the dustbins of history. What greater calamity could have befallen any people than the Shoah? Miraculously, from those ashes, the State of Israel rose after a national dispersion of two thousand years.

None of the above can mitigate the indescribable suffering that this small people has had to endure, nor can it lessen the guilt of those who brought the suffering upon them. How can one even dream of the justification of the Holocaust as the source for the establishment of the State of Israel? Perhaps this is a question which we will never be able to answer. We know from the Torah that when Jacob wrestled with the mystical angel that he was to be crowned with the new name of Israel. Prior to that great moment, however, he was struck in the thigh by that very angel, causing him to limp. It would seem, for reasons unbeknown, that before a great moment, there is a period of suffering. Just ask a mother who has given birth to a beloved child. Or note the Torah reading, "And there was evening and there was morning." The night precedes the dawn.

This, however, is a digression from our major point. The current terrorists and all their ilk should take note that no matter how much anguish they may cause, each and every one of their cowardly attacks will have one effect; it will forge Israel into an ever more united and stronger people.

Perhaps it would be fitting to close with the simple words from the Torah describing the results of the efforts of the first persecutors of the Jewish people.

"But as much as they would afflict them, so did they multiply and so did they gain strength" (Exodus 1:12).

Jewish Leadership

U nlike many other cultures, no leader in Jewish history, regardless how famous or great, has ever been accorded even the slightest degree of divinity. In fact, it is interesting and significant to note that many of those who rose to Jewish leadership were the least expected candidates. Although their inner strengths were phenomenal, their exterior qualities seemed to leave them extremely inadequate for their calling.

There may be a reason. No matter how great the leader, Jewish tradition has always taught us to look to God for our ultimate protection and leadership. Reaching all the way back to Abraham, our tradition teaches that Jewish historical events are not a series of disconnected happenings, but stepping-stones toward an ongoing destiny. Thus, Jewish leaders do not forge or create historical occurrences, but navigate their people through their challenges. Their external inadequacies may serve to reject the erroneous belief that human leadership is the last word in Jewish history.

The following three examples might serve to illustrate this theory.

The Torah informs us that Moses was the greatest prophet to ever have served the Jewish people. While this is certainly true, his exterior qualities hardly reflected this description. We know from the Torah itself that Moses continually declined God's mission because he felt himself totally inadequate to represent the Jewish people and lead them out of Egypt. Finally, when all else failed in his dialogue with God, he protested that he was *kvad peh* (heavy of speech). We are not certain of the exact meaning of these words, but they may have indicated a lisp or stutter. Now imagine Moses running for the office of President of the United States. How would his speeches have been received? Could he have been effective in leading the country? Yet, he achieved all his goals and arose to the distinction of being the greatest prophet. Clearly we see that there was a Greater Power whom he was representing.

A second example of the seemingly external inadequacy of a great Jewish leader is that of David, who not only was the king of Israel for many years, but also became the founder of the Davidic dynasty whose hereditary royalty will ultimately produce the Messiah. The biblical account of his anointment bears out his seeming inadequacy. We read how the prophet Samuel met with Jesse to inform him that he had been sent to anoint one of his sons to be the king of Israel. Although the name of the appointee had not been revealed to him, the prophet assured Jesse that he would recognize him once he laid his eyes upon him. The proud father paraded each of his seven sons before him. One was stronger and more powerful than the next. Each one was clearly fit to be the king of Israel, especially in those days when personal strength was essential. Yet, as they passed in front of the prophet, Samuel was forced to reject one after the other. Finally, Jesse stated that he had one more son. However, he was simply a lad who was a shepherd and played music on a lyre. How could he possibly be the king chosen to rule Israel and rid it of its enemies? Nevertheless, the prophet insisted on seeing him. His verdict was instantaneous. "This is the one whom God has chosen." Samuel took the anointing oil and poured it upon David's head. The message was clear; the eyes of God are not the eyes of man. Again, as in the case of Moses, the outward characteristics of David did not seem to indicate leadership qualities. Yet, under the guidance of God, David became a great king.

The final example, although there are many others, is that of Theodor Herzl. Of course, we are now dealing in the realm of political leadership, not to be confused with the lofty spiritual qualities of biblical personalities. Nevertheless, in the practical sphere of historical events, Theodor Herzl was a most unlikely candidate. Yet, he rose to the greatest of heights in succeeding to re-ignite the movement of the Jewish people back to their homeland. Both he and his parents were assimilated to the degree that Herzl was hardly aware of his Jewishness. The infamous Dreyfus case was a wake-up call for him. He publicly began to assert that there was no cure for European anti-Semitism. It was crucial that a homeland be established where Jewish teachings of justice and opportunity for all could be freely practiced. While there were others who began to preach political Zionism, it was Herzl who captured the imagination of the people who began to follow him to immediate action.

Theodore Herzl was born in 1860 and died in 1904. His accomplishments in only a fraction of his forty-four years are virtually beyond comparison. He was a driven man. He knew little about Jewish tradition and could not speak the Hebrew language. Yet, the facts cannot be denied.

He is accepted as the father of the State of Israel.

So we see that the quality of the Jewish leaders who were the most influential in forging the movement of Jewish history were seemingly the least likely ones to accomplish these goals. My purpose was to illustrate that there is a Higher Power that is ever-present in the passage of time and that His choices of leaders are perfect, a fact which invariably becomes apparent in retrospect.

The Land of Israel

The country which was originally known as Canaan was destined to be called the Land of Israel. In 1948, this name was given to the modern State of Israel. The history of the name goes back to the very beginnings of the Jewish people. In the book of Genesis, the episode of Jacob's wrestling with a mystical angel is described. After he succeeds in overcoming this apparition, Jacob's name was changed to Israel.

Since Jacob was the third generation of the Jewish people, it seems initially strange that the country should be named after him. After all, he was preceded by his grandfather Abraham and his father Isaac.

Upon reflection, however, one can discover very good cause for the land to be named after Israel. In no way does this detract from the honor due to his grandfather, Abraham and his father, Isaac. The reason for their names being passed over is, in my opinion, due to the family structure of Jacob's predecessors.

Abraham had two sons - Ishmael, father of the Arab nation, and Isaac. Throughout history, the Arab people have laid claim to this land. The contemporary struggle between the Jewish people of Israel and the Palestinians bears out this fact on the modern level, although the Arab claim existed throughout history. Had the country been called "Abraham," the Arabs would have had a valid entitlement to the land.

Now let us look at Isaac's family. He also had two sons, Jacob and Esau. Esau was the father of the Romans, whose descendants extended to Christianity and the gentile nations. They, too, asserted rights to what came to be known as Palestine. The Crusades are but one example of the fierceness with which they fought to conquer this land. Again, had the country been called "Isaac," they would have had a justifiable claim.

Jacob had many more children than his father and grandfather. Besides his daughter Dina, he had twelve sons. All of these children followed in the Jewish tradition and none of them originated any new cults or religions, as did their forebears.

Since this land was sworn by God to be the eternal homeland of the Jewish people, it is quite clear why it became known as the Land of Israel.

A Land Flowing with Milk and Honey

From the earliest description in the Torah, the Land of Israel has been referred to as the land of "milk and honey" (Exodus 3:18). With so many products for which Israel could be praised, one might wonder if there is something unique about these two items.

Upon closer examination, it emerges that both milk and honey have a common element. Honey is permitted to be eaten although it comes from non-kosher insects. Bees are forbidden to be eaten. There are many who claim that date honey is referred to in this analogy, but I am referencing honey which comes from bees.

The second item, milk, comes from the cow. Again, an enigma presents itself. Milk and meat are not allowed to be eaten together. A specific time must be allowed before dairy may be eaten after the consumption of meat, depending upon custom.

Which raises the interesting question whether these two items are simply poetic descriptions of the land or if there is a deeper message.

Frankly, I have never encountered a satisfactory explanation as to why Israel is compared to a land flowing with milk and honey or the fascinating fact that both emanate from conflicting sources.

One approach may be that the establishment of Israel and its progress is the result of many conflicting factors, internally and externally. Milk is the source of physical strength and sturdy posture. Honey is pleasant to the taste both when eaten by itself or in mixtures. Both products are in conflict with their sources, yet retain their individuality. This reflects many aspects of Israeli society. The citizenry of Israel reflect the Ingathering of the Exiles as foretold by our prophets centuries ago. They come from different and even conflicting societies, many of contradictory natures. Yet, almost miraculously, the integration is swift and almost total. Whenever I walk the streets of Israel and see so many different types all blended together, I feel that I am blessed to be a part of a large family.

Milk and honey may be extracted from conflicting origins, but in Israel they blend into a beautiful unity.

My Own Israel Miracle

I t happened quite some years ago, but I remember it vividly. My back had been hurting for an extended period of time, with the pain often reaching excruciating dimensions. The doctors explained that there was little they could do. Since I was human and walked on two legs, an undue pressure was exerted on a part of my back, which was the root of the problem. If I would have been a four-legged animal, the weight would have been more evenly distributed and all would have been well. Despite the pain, I chose not to walk on all fours.

During that period, I was scheduled to take one of my many visits to Israel. Throughout my Judaic studies, I often ran across wondrous stories about the Hot Springs of Tiberias. Some attributed the heat of the waters to the fact that they gushed out of the entrance of *"Gehenum"* (whose most appropriate translation would be "Hell"). The waters also had the reputation of possessing curative powers. I decided to test the waters. What did I have to lose?

A huge pool confronted me, with half the waters under the roof and the other half outside. Little fountains along the sides of the pool gushed up a constant flow of water.

I lay on one of the fountains for about ten minutes. The waters were warm and bubbled firmly on my back.

I dressed and returned home - and here is the point.

The pain in my back was gone and in all the following years, never came back until this very day.

I am not drawing any conclusions or making any assertions. I leave that up to you, the reader. But I do have some serious advice. If you should experience any pain or discomfort as I did, on your next trip to Israel, be sure to include Tiberias on your itinerary.

Lest We Forget

I t was Ralph Waldo Emerson (1803-1882) who said, "If the stars should appear but one night every thousand years, how man would marvel and stare."

I am constantly reminded of this adage as I walk along the streets of Jerusalem, Tel Aviv or any Israeli community. If anyone would have predicted how this country would spring to a new life a century ago, he would have been deemed a dreamer or a madman. Yet, because it is an ordinary daily experience, there is a tendency to take all this miraculous birth and development in one's stride. This is especially true of children who have never experienced pre-Israel, then known as Palestine. Just as the spectacular nightly appearance of the stars is all but taken for granted, so is the normal daily life of Israel.

Consider how the Hebrew language, which was restricted mainly to prayer and Jewish books of learning for centuries, quickly adapted itself to modern parlance and is now a functioning living mode of communication in every aspect of Israeli life.

The Israeli Defense Forces has become one of the most efficient and formidable armies in the world. They had little choice, but they rose to the challenge. Always prepared to thwart the attacks of surrounding countries steeped in deep and senseless hatreds against each other and especially against Israel, the IDF has become one of the most powerful armies in the world.

The economy and standard of living of Israel ranks higher than all its surrounding countries. It is among the highest in the world.

There is another element in the ever-growing strength of Israel. I refer to the educational and spiritual levels to which the country has risen. There are estimates that there are more *yeshivot* (schools of Torah learning) and *batei midrash* (study halls) than ever before in Jewish history.

I always feel a deep thrill when I hear Hebrew being spoken all around me by people whose varied appearances reflect the Ingathering of the Exiles. After two thousand years of wandering and living in constant minority and persecuted status, it would have been an amazing feat for the Jewish people to have just survived. But to build a modern and efficient country in only seven decades is truly miraculous.

Which brings me back to the above observation of Ralph Waldo Emerson. The fact that modern Israel's birth and growth is an everyday and evolving process could mitigate the awareness of the ongoing miracle and we run the risk of taking things for granted. That would be a huge and sad mistake. We must treat the development and continuing thriving of Israel as a miracle beyond comparison. If it would have all happened in a short period of time, people would marvel and hardly believe it. Time and constant progress must never be allowed to detract from the huge and ongoing miracle.

King David expressed it succinctly, "When God brought back the exiles of Zion, we were like people caught in a dream" (Psalms 126).

But it is not a dream; it is a blessed reality.

One Big Family

It was just a minor incident, but it revealed so much. As another possible conflict was developing between Israel and its Arab antagonists, a looming danger arose for Israel of chemical attacks. Everyone was urged to pick up gas masks at their local civil defense headquarters. My granddaughter, Nava, still a little girl at the time (she is now the mother of two), was emphatically resisting the procedure of trying on the mask and was making her displeasure well-known.

A young soldier who was picking up his own gas mask, noticed the situation. He walked over to Nava and asked her if she would help him get his mask on. She agreed and after this task was completed, he asked her if she would let him help get hers on. She again agreed and the "crisis" was over.

Just one big family.

OBSERVATIONS

"If you would like to think about numbers, consider how many snowflakes it takes to produce a huge blizzard. Then marvel at the fact that each snowflake is reputed to have its own unique shape and design." (Rabbi Norbert Weinberg)

Sitting in the House of God

I arrived at the synagogue quite some time before the services were scheduled to begin. Being a regular congregant, I had the distinct advantage of knowing the combination which opened the front door, which meant that I would not have to wait outside in the cold. It was late in the day when I entered the Sanctuary. The sun had already descended and there were few windows to give any light. As a result, the hall was steeped in darkness. It was too early for any arrivals and I found myself completely alone. The only source of illumination was the rays cast by the *Ner Tamid* (the Eternal Light) positioned over the Holy Ark. I was not acquainted with the intricacies of turning on the lights.

As I settled into my regular seat, my first impulse was to reach for a neighboring book – any book – to take up the time. I quickly realized that my attempts to make out the words in the dark were an exercise in futility. I thought of fiddling with my cell phone, but there was nothing of even the remotest interest there. It quickly dawned on me that I had no choice but to sit in my seat and wait for people to enter and the services to begin.

Just to sit and do nothing? That seemed to be the height of awkwardness. I felt the need to do something, even if only to listen to the backdrop blaring of a radio or television. As I sat contemplating this dilemma, the rays of the *Ner Tamid* seemed to shine brighter and focus directly upon me. I stared at them as if in a hypnotic state. A rare feeling of inner calm enveloped me as I drifted into a state of spiritual tranquility.

It occurred to me that even though I recite Psalm 145 – "*Ashrei yoshvei vetecha*" - that contains the words of joyful fulfillment at "sitting in the house of God" three times each day, its meaning never really dawned on me until that moment. It is not necessary to always be doing, doing and doing. There are richly rewarding moments when one does nothing but sit and rediscover one's inner self.

When the lights went on, I felt richly renewed and fulfilled. I had been privileged to truly experience the joy of "sitting in the house of God."

Something Does Not Compute

A student in a yeshiva confided the following to his friend.

"I was doing my best to concentrate during the *Amida* (silent prayer), but could not help noticing one of the greatest sages of our day, standing in prayer next to me. I was totally intimidated for the rest of the service."

His friend looked at him in wonder. "You were standing before our Heavenly Father and you were intimidated by a rabbi?"

Mirror, Mirror on The Wall

There are many areas in Jewish tradition in which mirrors play a prominent role. One teaching states that a mirror is, after all, primarily composed of glass and one should be able to look through it and see as far as his eyes will allow. It is only when a metal such as mercury intervenes that one is left with seeing nothing but - oneself! It takes only a small amount of precious metal to turn one inward and see only his own reflection.

It is a well-known fact that mirrors are covered in the home during the seven-day period of mourning (*Shiva*). The practical reason for this custom is that it could be shocking and painful for a mourner to suddenly see himself in the shabby attire and state of dishevel in which mourners find themselves.

There is, however, a more novel and perhaps, deeper explanation. A mirror is extremely fickle. As long as the person stands before it, the image is fully displayed. As soon as the person moves away, the image disappears and is no more. By covering the mirrors, we are making the statement that, in this respect, we are very different. The fact that the person whom we are mourning is no longer physically with us in no way diminishes his/her spiritual presence.

But all this is introductory to another somewhat new mirror usage. It has become very accepted for people who are donning their *tefillin* (phylacteries) to utilize a hand mirror with which they ascertain that the box placed on the forehead is in the exact place where Jewish law instructs - between one's eyes. It is almost amusing to watch how some people, with constricted brow, stare intently into the mirror to carefully scrutinize the

222

exact position of this box. Only when they are totally satisfied is the mirror replaced and the prayers commence.

It is important that I make it perfectly clear that I have the greatest respect and admiration for anyone who seeks to improve and enhance his manner of worship. For myself, however, I find this utilization of the mirror somewhat puzzling. This entire "ritual" is of relatively recent vintage. My father and his generation never, to the best of my knowledge, heard of it. For myself, I know exactly where my hairline is, where my two eyes converge with my nose and the width of my forehead. What further benefit could a mirror possibly offer?

If I may be allowed a moment of innocent humor, I would suggest that a standing mirror be placed on the dining room table in order to guide the forks and spoons into the mouth!

The Power of Possession

The engaging story is told of a group of Russians who were being inducted into Communist philosophy prior to the Bolshevik revolution. A commissar was questioning one of the group in the hope of eliciting the proper responses.

"Now tell me," he asked. "What would you do if you owned two homes?"

"I would keep one and give the other to my comrade."

"Excellent!" the commissar beamed to a round of applause.

"Let me ask you this," he continued. "What if you were the owner of two automobiles? What would you do?"

The immediate reply was similar. "I would keep one car and give the other to a comrade."

"You are a true Communist," the commissar responded happily. "So here is my final question. How would you proceed if you were in possession of two shirts?"

"I would keep them," was the firm response.

"This is very curious," the commissar wondered. "Why are your actions so different with two shirts?"

"Because I own two shirts."

It is amazing how volumes and volumes of philosophy can be reduced to a few simple words.

Gesundheit

In Western culture, a burp is somewhat frowned upon and the guilty party will usually excuse himself. A hiccup is generally disregarded or perhaps greeted with a chuckle. No attention is paid to a normal cough. Not so a sneeze. This physical phenomenon is accepted in a positive manner as long as the one who sneezes covers his nose or sneezes into his elbow to prevent the possible spread of germs. In fact, this physical outburst is greeted with wishes of good health.

In France, the response is *"a votre santé."* In Hebrew, it is *"labriyut"* – "to your health." The German response is *"Gesundheit."*

There is a fascinating Midrash which seeks to give a reason for these responses to a sneeze.

It is in the book of Genesis that we are first introduced to the practice of making preparations for death. Prior to Jacob, people simply lived a certain period of time and then died. The Midrash states that Jacob was the first person who requested of God to reveal to him the general time of his impending death. Apparently this wish was granted and we learn that Joseph, his son, was alerted to the fact that Jacob had become ill. Joseph then took his two children, Jacob's grandsons, and brought them to the elder for a blessing. We read further that Jacob blessed all his children prior to his death. He also made provisions with his son, Joseph, that he would be buried in the Land of Israel with his forefathers.

How did people die before Jacob? They died as the result of a sneeze, states the Midrash. There was no warning or preconditions. A person simply sneezed and died. I have even heard the claim that in the interim of the split second of a sneeze, the bodily functions momentarily cease.

Whether scientifically sustainable or an intriguing page of folklore, this is the Midrashic response as to why people of many cultures greet the sneeze with good wishes for health.

Easy Does It

It was a major gathering of a Chasidic sect. Hundreds of *Chasidim*, garbed in black suits and hats, sat at long tables in front of their Rebbe who, surrounded by his intimate entourage, smiled benignly and occasionally raised his silver cup to extend his blessings and greetings.

At various intervals, he regaled his devoted disciples with insights into Torah and *Kabbala* (mysticism). As soon as he completed a discourse, the throng broke into joyous song. Drinks and delicacies befitting the holy Shabbat were heaped on the tables which were covered with white tablecloths. The surface of the tables buckled as fists smashed upon them to the cheerful rhythm of the melodies.

The huge crowd sang and shouted, clapped their hands and stomped their feet, with great enthusiasm.

Suddenly, a young man, apparently unable to contain his zeal, jumped on top of the table and began to dance in front of the Rebbe in an apparently uncontrollable trance of fervor and ecstasy. His long black beard swung in the air as he waved his arms in an ever-increasing rush of elation. His stomping feet shook the table as the dishes rattled and seemed ready to fly in every direction.

"*Nu*," one of the disciples respectfully asked the Rebbe, as he gazed in admiration at the young man. "What do you think of Yankel's enthusiasm?"

The Rebbe was quiet for a long moment of contemplation. "I think," he finally replied, "that Yankel should sit down and finish his *cholent*."

Old or New

I t is fascinating how a chance detail can trigger a memory. As I was scanning the books in my library, a *siddur* (Hebrew prayer book) caught my attention. It had been given to me by the grandson of a very favorite relative who lived in a charming Israeli settlement by the name of *Kfar Haroeh* and had recently passed away. The book always brought back fond memories and has much sentimental value. However, the pages were well-used and the entire volume was not in very good shape.

It brought to mind an incident which occurred many years ago when my trips to Israel were just beginning. On one of these trips, we joined a busload of tourists. Sights and events were explained to us by the tour guide who regaled us with many facts and stories. This particular excursion was highlighted by a visit to the city of Safed where we entered an ancient synagogue. After relating all the pertinent history of this structure, the guide called our attention to the prayer books lining the rows of seats. They were extremely old and worn from decades of use.

We were told how, during one of those trips, an apparently wealthy tour member, expressed dismay at the poor condition of these books. If he would be informed of the purchase price of an entirely new set, he would be honored to subsidize the full amount. Although everyone was duly impressed, the guide was scandalized.

"What?" he exclaimed. "Replace these holy books? Of course I know you meant well, but do you have any idea of the tears, hopes and prayers that permeate these pages? They are priceless! They can never be replaced with new ones."

Apparently, this little exchange always remained in the back of my mind and I fully appreciate its import. Nevertheless, while I cherish sacred books of family vintage, I prefer those which I utilize on a daily basis to be reasonably new and clean. As a result, when any one of mine gets frayed and worn, I make my way to the book store and purchase a new one.

THE ANIMAL WORLD

"If one person tells you that you have the ears of a donkey, pay no attention to him. If two people tell you, prepare a saddle for yourself." (*Midrash Rabba; Bereshit* 45)

A Personal Concern

While the majesty and beauty of the Yom Kippur service in the Holy Temple (*Avoda*) is awe-inspiring, I continue to be troubled by one of its components. I refer to the goat that was sent into the wilderness, bearing the sins of the people. It is from this ritual that the name "scapegoat" evolved.

The Torah describes how this ceremony was to be conducted. We read in the Book of Leviticus (Chapter 16) how two identical goats were brought before the High Priest (*Kohen Gadol*). Two lots were placed upon the animals: one was destined for God (*Hashem*) and the other for *Azazel*. The former was sacrificed as a sin-offering (*chatat*), while the latter was to be sent into the wilderness.

At some point, it developed that this hapless animal was taken to a steep cliff, from which it was hurled to its death. The Talmud (Tractate *Yoma*) recounts in detail how, struggling and thrashing, the goat was sliced into pieces by the jagged rocks as it plummeted from the high mountain.

Please do not misunderstand me. I am sure that the sages who ordained this form of execution had their reasons. Sometimes we are not furnished with the full picture. The somewhat disturbing aspect is that the requirement for this live goat to be pushed to its painful death is not spelled out in the Torah. Biblically, we are only commanded that it be sent into the wilderness, symbolically bearing the sins of the Jewish people.

The difficulty I have with this matter is predicated upon a wealth of commandments and traditions which guard and protect the animal world. Balaam was rebuked for beating his donkey; the mother bird must be sent away before her eggs are removed from the nest; an ox may not be muzzled when pulling its load; to state but a few examples.

There are those who maintain that no conclusions may be drawn from the above examples. They assert that anyone who feels that these commandments demonstrate God's compassion are in error. Each commandment (*mitzva*), they teach, must be understood in and of itself, and any attempt to derive a further purpose is fraught with the dangers of error.

While there may be general merit to this school of thought, I nevertheless find it difficult to understand the treatment of this goat in the face of all the apparently contradicting examples which, I believe, reflect our position on this matter. To hurl this ill-fated goat off a jagged cliff appears to contradict so many commandments on this subject, just a few of which I have listed above. Perhaps further study of the matter may provide me with more insight.

Breakfast with a Kitten

U nlike the British, Israelis do not generally exhibit a great fondness for cats. These felines congregate around the garbage receptacles which line the streets at measured intervals. Essentially, they are scavengers. They basically avoid people and are treated with equal disdain. I have personally always liked cats and have had a few as pets in the past. They require a minimum of care.

I make these comments because I was recently having breakfast on the patio in Efrat, when a kitten sauntered up to my table and greeted me with a sorrowful "meow." Now that was most unusual because, as I mentioned, cats simply do not approach people in Israel. My immediate reaction was one of some guilt. Here I was eating a hearty breakfast while this little feline seemed to be informing me that it was hungry.

I remembered an explicit Torah imperative, "And you shall give to your cattle and you shall eat and be satisfied" (Deuteronomy 8:10). Clearly one is instructed to first feed one's animals and only afterwards to eat to one's satisfaction. Technically, the verse states "your cattle" and since the kitten was not mine, I did not have any actual responsibility toward its sustenance. Nevertheless, I was having a satisfying meal and a hungry kitten was meowing at me.

I dragged myself out of my chair, walked to the freezer and extracted a tuna nugget which I warmed in the microwave and placed before the kitten. After returning to my breakfast, the kitten ate the nugget, licking up every crumb. Then, with a touch of Israeli *chutzpa,* it jumped up on my table to determine what else was available. I believe that a line had been crossed, so I gave the kitten a gentle swish with my newspaper and off it went.

Thus went my breakfast with an Israeli kitten.

Lessons from the Animal World

J ewish tradition teaches that all animals serve varying functions which benefit mankind and can even serve as an example. Thus, the buzzing of the mosquito will awaken a slumbering person, especially if he is studying the Torah. The cat teaches us modesty because it seeks a secluded spot when it takes care of its bodily functions and then carefully covers its waste. The dog is known for its loyalty, wolves for living in community and certain birds for how well they care for their young.

King Solomon focuses on the ant in the Book of Proverbs (6: 6): "Go to the ant, lazy one. Consider her ways and become wise." The industry of the ant is phenomenal. It seems that their main efforts are to store up food in the summer for the winter season. Watching them as they methodically go about their tasks and dig elaborate tunnels can certainly be an inspiration for people to stop procrastinating and get their jobs done.

A thought occurred to me regarding the squirrel, which I have never come across in our literature. Especially in the fall season, we see squirrels scurrying in a determined and industrial manner with little nuts in their mouths, busily digging small crevices in which they deposit these morsels and then carefully replace the earth. I highly doubt that the squirrels will be able to later find the holes where they deposited the nuts. This is the height of unselfish living. These little rodents are all engaged in a communal effort to help feed each other. While the original intent may be self-serving, the entire venture is one of genuine altruism. This is certainly a characteristic to be emulated by mankind and is a wonderful example of how people can be of great help to one another.

Another striking characteristic which I have observed in the animal world is the complete absence of any form of hypocrisy. Man has the ability to say one thing while meaning exactly the opposite, resulting in much misery and strife. Not so in the animal world whose members are simply incapable of expressing one emotion while feeling another.

One sunny day, I was walking down the street after synagogue services and passed some trees where hundreds of birds were resting during their migration to a distant destination. They were all chirping and twittering loudly. It was quite a symphony. It then occurred to me that they were engaged in exactly the same activity that I had experienced just a few moments earlier. They clearly seemed to be extolling their Maker and vocalizing their joy if for no other reason than to express thanks for being alive on such a beautiful day. If you think me foolish for these musings, please consider the concluding words of King David in Psalms (150:6): "Let everything that has breath praise God."

It would appear that we are just one component of the entire universe, each of which praises God in its own unique manner.

Yes, we have much to learn from the animal world!

Final Thought

"May the Lord bless you from Zion; may you see the good of Jerusalem all the days of your life; and may you live to see your children's children. Peace be on Israel!" (Psalms 128)

אילן אילן במה אברכך?

יהי רצון שכל נטיעות
שנוטעין ממך יהיו כמותך!

"Tree, tree, with what should I bless you? ...May it be God's will that all the trees planted from your seeds should be like you!" (Talmud Taanit 5b) Rabbi Norbert Weinberg pictured with his great-grandchildren, ken yirbu, may they continue to grow and flourish!

Of Children and Peace

"And you shall see children to your children,
peace upon Israel" (Psalms 128:6).

What connection is there between children and peace? Upon reflection, the awareness emerges that one is directly related to the other. We know how many children tragically die in war, persecution and other disasters, bereaving the former generation of the joy of seeing their children becoming their descendants. It is only in a peaceful society that one generation gives durable birth and life to the next generation.

Another aspect of this prerequisite is peace in the home. Without this condition, there is strife, divorce and either an absence of children or children so marred by their environment that they can bring no happiness or the assurance of any meaningful future.

The blessing inherent in this verse is of the greatest magnitude. When Israel will live in peace, internally and externally, it will enjoy all the blessings of peace and a happy future.

Printed in the United States
By Bookmasters